The Left-Handers' Handbook

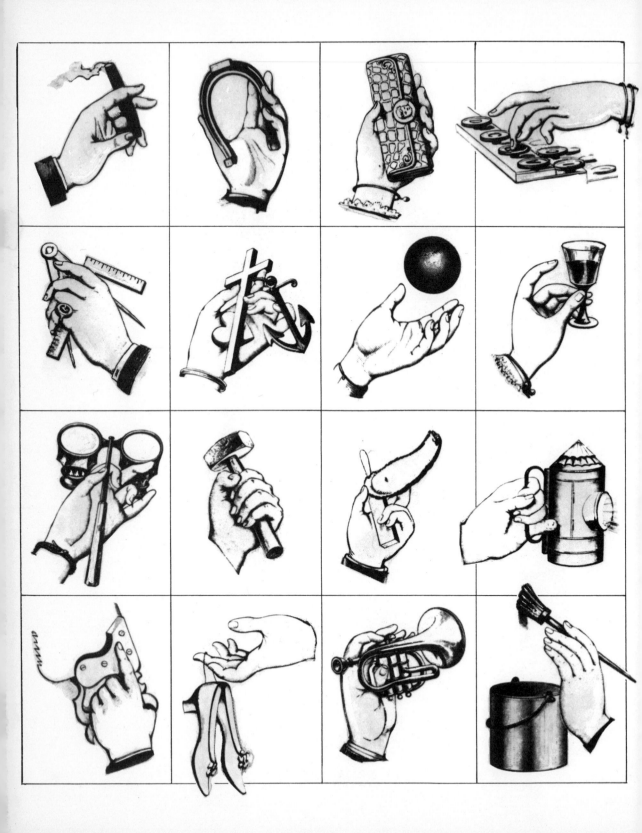

The Left-Handers' Handbook

James Bliss & Joseph Morella

Edited by
Ann Novotny

A & W VISUAL LIBRARY

NEW YORK

First published in the United States of America in 1980 by
A & W Publishers, Inc.
95 Madison Avenue
New York, New York 10016
By arrangement with Communication Ventures Inc.

Design and illustrations by Robert H. Yahn
Picture research by Research Reports, New York

Library of Congress Catalog Card Number: 78-71038
ISBN: 0-89104-133-8
Printed in the United States of America

Contents

The Empress Josephine, her left hand (as seen by a palmist), and her left-handed husband, Napoleon.

Introduction

This is a book about the joys and tribulations of being left-handed. It is filled with history and folklore, with science and speculation. It offers sensible advice to "lefties" on how to overcome the aggravations of a right-handed world and how to enjoy the advantages of membership in a most distinguished and interesting minority group.

We hope to give you cause to be glad, if you are left-handed. And if you are right-handed, we hope to give you fresh appreciation of the lefties you may be lucky enough to share your friendship, life or work with. We wish to surprise you, to share new information with you, and to make you laugh.

We offer you an even-handed survey of what is now known about that singular condition called sinistrality. Is it a habit caused by genetics, brain structure or social environment? Are gorillas and chimpanzees left-handed or right-handed? And why? We try to answer these questions and others you may never have thought of.

Left-handedness has implications far beyond a simple preference for doing most things with the left hand. Recent research suggests that left-handers are more creative, more adaptable, and better suited to certain occupations than the majority of right-handed people in the world. In general, there are more advantages to being left-handed than you may think.

If you are a lefty, you already know about the disadvantages. Every ordinary corkscrew, potato peeler and watch-stem conspires to make simple chores more irksome for you. Gum wrappers open from the right. Pencil sharpeners, scissors, cameras and golf clubs are not designed for you, but for righties. Subway turnstiles, phone booths (even telephones at home) and revolving doors all favor the right-handed. In the workshop (power saws and drills) and in the recreation room (playing cards), the lefty is forgotten. No left-handed one-arm bandits exist in Las Vegas. Unless guitars and other stringed instruments are re-strung, they favor right-handed musicians. Directions and teaching instructions for every hobby and skill, from writing to shorthand and knitting, are designed for right-handers. Dials on television sets, radios and other electronic instruments all turn to suit the righty. You may be used to the fact that the gear-shift lever in your car is at your right (unless you are lucky enough to live and drive in Great Britain), but do you know that as an airplane pilot, left-handed, the demands on you will be doubly demanding because most controls are on your right? Certain office machines can be operated only with the right hand (the typewriter seems to be the only truly unbiased machine: in fact, many of the most frequently used letters and symbols are at your left). You are not paranoid if you believe that job discrimination exists: hundreds of complaints have been registered against employers reluctant to hire lefties.

You may be startled, if you are right-handed, to learn how unfair, even discriminatory, our society is toward those who are left-handed. This plight of the lefty is nothing new . . . or is it? A cross-cultural survey of the history of hand preference reveals facts that are curiously contradictory. Zuni Indians (in what is today the southwestern United States) believe that the left is the older and wiser of our two sides. But the Bible repeatedly equates left-handedness with evil, right-handedness with good and God.

Language can betray our deepest prejudices. What are the origins of words such as *sinister*, *righteous* or the *left-handed compliment*? In French, *gauche* means *left*—and *awkward* or *tactless*. The Italian terms for *left* and *left-handedness* are *mancino* and *mancini*, also meaning *defective*, *maimed* or *deceitful*, and the three famous Mancini sisters attached to the French court of Louis XIV are remembered by French and Italian historians for their involvement in the sinister (well, it really was) Poison Affair of 1680.

The ancient Greeks, those sensible people, had a better word for left-handed: *aristera*, which also meant *best* (as in *aristocratic*). They and the Zuni Indians are not the only peoples to believe that the left side implies special and good powers. If you are a lefty, and proud of it, you are not alone. To start with, chances are high that you know many other lefties personally. Left-handedness tends to be inherited in families, so some of your sisters and brothers, parents, aunts and uncles, and your own children, too, may very well be "southpaws." Being left-handed yourself, you also are apt to notice and to meet other lefties—because you are particularly observant about which hand your friends and co-workers use for eating, writing and for everyday tasks. If you are right-handed, it is almost impossible for you not to have at least a few left-handed friends, acquaintances and co-workers: ten or perhaps even fifteen percent of the American population is supposed to be left-handed. And that statistic is assumed to include only those people who *write* with their left hand. Millions more perform daily tasks ambidexterously or with their left hand, but are accepted as "righties" simply because as children they were taught (or compelled to learn) to use their right hand for writing.

Many readers may remember

that they felt naturally left-handed as children but were taught in school to write with their right (yes, "right") hand. Today, most children in western European countries and in the United States are allowed to use the hand of their natural preference. Since this was not the custom in the recent past, or in many other countries, it is almost impossible for statisticians to determine how many lefties really exist in the population of any nation.

Is your child left-handed? Don't be concerned ... be interested. Parents used to believe that their offspring should be encouraged or forced to use their right hands, because in the long run it would be easier to be right-handed in a right-handed world. But, even in the past, the accomplishments of some intractable lefties have left the rest of the right-handed world in awe. In this book, you will meet Leonardo da Vinci, Harpo Marx, Harry Truman, Babe Ruth, and many, many other famous lefties. You will read that Ravel, Prokofiev and Britten have composed some piano music for the left hand only. And you will find practical help at hand (whichever) in our list of organizations lefties may join, shops they may visit, and products they may buy through special mail-order catalogs.

Unfortunately, we cannot do anything about the fact that—when you write away for these products, catalogs and newsletters—the post office will require you to stick the stamp in the upper *right*-hand corner of the envelope.

Marie Mancini (whose name means "left"—and "deceitful"), found guilty in the Poison Affair of 1680.

The Bible repeatedly equates left-handedness with evil, right-handedness with good and God.

MARCEL MARCEAU • LEONARDO DA VINCI • HARPO MARX • KIM NOVAK

Our Right-Handed Society

[OR IS IT ?]

BENJAMIN FRANKLIN • PELE • DOROTHY HAMILL • MARK SPITZ

What do the words really mean...

[ARE YOU "SINISTER" OR "DEXTEROUS"?]

"What's in a word? . . ." The answer is almost everything. And you don't need to be an etymologist, a specialist in the origin and development of words, to see that in English and almost every other language the words used for left and left-handedness are (to put this mildly) unflattering, unkind and underhanded.

In our language, the word *left* denotes the side opposite the right. Even this simple definition can be phrased to sound like a criticism: *The Oxford English Dictionary* defines *left* as "the distinctive epithet of the hand which is normally the weaker of the two. . . ." Left may also mean *abandoned* or *leftover* as unwanted remnants, while *left-handed* is *awkward, maladroit, derisive, dubious* and *insincere. Right*, on the other hand, as a synonym for *just, legal, moral, fitting* or *proper* (as in, "It is not right to tell lies"), *favorable* and *desirable* (as in "Now is the right time to act"), *satisfactory, sane* or *normal* (as in, "She is in her right

mind again"), and—as a noun—a *privilege* or *prerogative*. The *right side* of the cloth is the side meant to be worn outwards, facing observers. To *right* a boat means to set it in an upright and proper position. And to *right* a wrong is to make amends or reparations.

How can privileged righties make any amends to the English-speaking lefties who, for centuries, have had to cope with subtle discrimination in our most basic form of communication, our language? This verbal unfairness dates all the way back to Anglo-Saxon times—the fifth and sixth centuries—when Germanic tribes invaded and settled in Britain and changed its language. *Left* derives from their Old English word *lyft* or *lefte*, meaning *weak* or *worthless.* The peculiar illness *lyft-adl* was "left-disease," *paralysis.* Our word *right*, too, comes from the Old English *riht*, meaning *straight* and *erect, just* and *correct.*

Dozens of phrases have evolved during the following fifteen hundred years, all using *left* or *left-handed* to connote the wrong, evil, shady or undesirable alternative to right. *Left-handed flattery* is insincere, and a *left-handed compliment* may in fact be a put-down. If you *don't know left from right*, you are confused or stupid; if you have *two left feet*, you are clumsy; and if you *go over to the left*, you turn good into bad. The *left hand of Fortune* brings bad luck, and the *left hand of a friend* symbolizes betrayal, possibly by someone who drank a *left-handed toast* to you, wishing you ill. With all this malevolence directed

A left-hand honeymoon is an escapade with someone else's spouse.

If you marry with the left hand, you marry a person below your own social position.

A left-handed toast wishes you ill.

The dictionary defines "left" as "the distinctive epithet of the hand which is normally the weaker of the two."

If someone calls you "ambidextrous," you are being complimented for being skillfully right-handed on both sides (like this Pennsylvania folk-art soldier).

A child of the left hand is an illegitimate baby.

The "sinister" or left hand came to symbolize evil.

14

"Right" is a synonym for "just," "legal," "moral." As a noun, it means a privilege or prerogative. (The coat of arms of Charles II of England, 1660).

"Aristocrat."

"Sinister."

at you, you may well feel that you're way *out in left field*, lost and off-base. You might seek solace in a *left-hand honeymoon*—an escapade with someone else's spouse. But if you *marry with the left hand*, you will be marrying a person below your social position, while a *left-handed marriage* is not really a marriage at all, and one that might result in a *child of the left hand*, an illegitimate baby. As if things weren't already bad enough at home, out in the world a *left-footer* is a Protestant in a Catholic majority—and a Catholic in a Protestant society.

Centuries before the invading Anglo-Saxons brought all this prejudice into the English langauge, the ancient Greeks—from whom we derive some good words—were kinder to lefties. The Greek word *aristera*, meaning *left*, also referred to *the best*, as in *aristocratic*. Unfortunately, when the Romans conquered Greece, they supplanted the Greek tongue with Latin, and the future of lefties in language began to look dim. The Latin word for *right* is *dexter*, and the Romans were pro-right to the point of compulsion. Perhaps because the Romans had learned to use their right hands well enough to conquer most of the known world, the word *dexterous*, handed down to us, has come to mean *skillful*, *adroit* and *clever*.

If you are a lefty who has learned to use both hands with equal skill, are you flattered if someone calls you *ambidextrous?* Look at that word again: its root is *dexter*, and actually you are being complimented for being as skillful as a right-handed person on both sides. (To remind you of this subtle insult implicit in the origin of the word, we will use the less usual but alternative spelling, *ambidexterous*, throughout this book). And here's the kicker: *ambidexterous* may also mean *double-dealing, deceitful, hypocritical.*

The Romans' word for *left* was *sinister*, exactly the same word used today in both English and French. It derived from *sinus*, Latin for *pocket*, because Romans always had the pockets of their togas on the left side. And since the Romans were champions of the right hand—saluting each other with their right hands, shaking hands with the right, showing that they held no weapon in that hand—they soon came to think of the left hand as being used for covert purposes. *Sinister* came to mean *hidden, sneaky, under-handed,* even *evil*, the meanings it has to this day.

The Romans started a trend of linguistic discrimination against lefties, and this discrimination exists today in almost every major language. To start with languages most familiar to us, look at Spanish, spoken not only in Spain but in most of Latin America and many regions of the United States. *Zurdo* means left-handed . . . and *malicious*. Worse, it may also mean *going in the wrong direction*. And the phrase *no ser zurdo*, literally meaning *don't be left-handed*, really implies *don't be stupid!*

The Italian language is no kinder. The words for *left* and *left-handedness* are *mancino* and *mancini*, also meaning *defective, maimed*, even *deceitful*. Another Italian term referring to left-handedness is *stanca*, which may be translated as *fatigued*.

In German, as in Dutch, the word for *left* is *link*. The Germans use the term *linkisch* for someone awkward, and their word for *right* is *recht*, meaning *good, true* and *just*. Look around the rest of Europe: things don't get any better. In Portugese, *canhoto* refers not only to left-handedness, but also means *weak* and *mischievous*. The Russians call lefties *levja*, and they use a related term, *na levo*, to describe sneakiness. Even in Romany, the language of the gypsies, the word for left-handed, *bongo*, is derogatory: it also means *evil* or *crooked*.

In French, *gauche*, the word for *left*, originally meant *bent*. It has come to mean *clumsy, awkward, socially inept*, and the word and its subsidiary meanings have been incorporated into English. So has the French word *droit*, or *right:* in English, we say *adroit*, meaning *skillful*.

People in all countries speak informally. Colloquial language, or slang, is often their preference. Unhappily, slang terms from Britain, Australia and Germany have contributed to the bad linguistic view of lefties.

Widdershins or *withershins* is an adverb describing actions done in the wrong direction, in reverse, or counter-clockwise, in a direction opposite to that of the sun. This is another term once applied in a derogatory sense to left-handedness. It comes down to us as a slang term

In French, "gauche" means "left."

"Sinister" was the word of the anti-left Romans.

In the language of the gypsies, the word for "left-handed" also means "evil" or "crooked."

In Spanish, "zurdo" means left-handed . . . and malicious.

derived from medieval German, meaning, literally, "against the journey" (of the sun). The sun, if you stand facing it in the south, rises on your left (in the east) and sets on your right (in the west), and seems therefore to be turning in a clockwise direction. And the sun was the first object of worship in primitive societies. So it's easy to see that going against the direction of the sun-god would appear to be unlucky, unnatural and evil. It is from German that we get the word wiederschein, counter-clockwise, from which this slang term originates. Going counter-clockwise, or spiralling to the left, was once considered to be the method of the Devil and his brood—witches and warlocks who defied the laws of God and of nature. Since the Middle Ages, the term *widdershins* has lost its connotation of sinister activity. It is now simply a colloquial term for left-handedness, and it is no longer derogatory to point out that a person is doing something "widdershins."

Hayfoot-Strawfoot is another slang term, rarely used today, but in times past applied to lefties. It started in 18th-century Europe. The King of Prussia, Frederick William I (1688-1740), known as the Soldier-King, decided that he needed a more disciplined army. The practice of marching with the right foot first had prevailed for many hundreds of years, in fact, ever since the Romans had made a practice of always entering a house with the right foot first. "Let's change the marching orders," thought old Frederick. "That will shake them up and shape them up."

It did. To this day, as everyone of us who has ever marched in a parade knows, marching is one of the few activities where left comes first. It's *Left*, right, *left*, right, *hup* ...2...3...4... *left* ... *left* ...."

The disciplined Prussians learned this quickly. But as the custom spread slowly across Europe and to America, the less well disciplined (and possibly denser) righties in the armies of other countries had difficulty mastering the new drill. One bright officer came up with an idea.

"Hayfoot-Strawfoot."

Since most of his recruits were farmboys from rural backgrounds, he ordered hay (soft grass cut and dried for fodder) placed in their left boots, and straw (prickly stalks of threshed grain) placed in their right boots. Being country boys, his soldiers could tell the difference at once, and the marching orders were changed to "*Hayfoot*, strawfoot ... *hayfoot*, strawfoot. ...." Although *hayfoot* should refer only to lefties, and *strawfoot* to righties, somehow the entire *hayfoot-strawfoot* term has, over the years, been retained to describe only the lefties. And that seems hardly fair, since it was a phrase invented to help the dim-witted righties who found it difficult to march with their left foot first.

The most common British slang term is perhaps the most offensive. *Cack* is British slang for excrement (in France and America, the word is *caca*), and long ago the British began calling lefties *cack-handers*. It's easy to trace the origin of this. Moslems eat with their right hands, dipping into a communal bowl; they reserve their left hands for cleaning themselves. When British Crusaders came into contact with the Moslems of the Middle Ages, they adopted the Moslem attitude toward the "unclean" hand. Today, *cack-handed* in British slang has come to mean *shady* or *dishonest*. Most people who use the word have no idea of its origin or of its implicit insult to all left-handers. Other vulgar British words for lefties include *spuddy-handed*, *cork-handed*, *cat-handed* and *bang-handed*.

Australians use an apparently charming, but really derogatory, slang term for a lefty ... a *molly-dooker*. A *molly* is a young girl, or an effeminate man, while *dooker* is a derivative of *dukes*, or fists. So, literally, *molly-dooker* may be translated as *woman-handed* or, more precisely, as *sissy-fisted*. Well, we are all aware that a number of famous pugilists, including the legendary Gentleman Jim Corbett, would have put up their dukes (left and right) to challenge any Aussie foolish enough to call them sissy-fisted. And would anyone dare to call karate champion Bill Wallace a molly-dooker?

"Portsider."

The Arabic custom of the unclean hand gave us the offensive word "cack-hander."

An Australian "molly-dooker" is a "sissy-fisted" lefty.

Portsider is another term not in general usage. But it is an old word now being promoted by many "lefties" as an acceptable alternative name. The word comes from the *port* or left side of a ship or aircraft (the right side is the starboard). The nautical term *starboard* can be traced to the fact that in early ships the apparatus with which to *steer* the vessel was always on the right side. To keep the rudder free, therefore, a ship always docked with its left side—originally called *larboard* or *ladde-borde* because it was the side for the lading or loading of the cargo—against the dock. But captains discovered that the sound of "larboard" was easily confused with "starboard" in their shouted commands; the confusion was ended by naming the left side of the ship the *portside*.

Whether or not *portsider* catches on as a generally used term, one acceptable alternative to *lefty* does enjoy popularity, and that's the American slang word *southpaw*. Boxing and baseball both claim that the term originated in their sporting circles. Remember the scene in the film "Rocky," where the fighter explains the meaning of the word to his girl? Boxing doesn't have a solid claim to the word, however: the truth is that the term originated in baseball and was quickly picked up by boxers.

A Chicago sportswriter—possibly Charles Seymour of the old *Herald*—is credited with coining the word back in the 1890s. The old Chicago baseball park on the West Side was built (as are most major-league parks) so that the sun would not shine into the batter's eyes. The batter faced east or northeast, confronting the pitcher who faced west or southwest. When the pitcher was left-handed, he used the hand that was on the south side of the park. Cold winds that blew across Chicago may have made its residents acutely conscious of direction; in any case, the townsfolk already favored the term "Southside" for the area of their city that lay in that direction. Then an inventive sportswriter used an instantly-recognizable geographic term to coin a new word for a left-handed pitcher: *southpaw*.

Like the unknown soldier, this unknown writer should be given a special place of honor. *Southpaw* has become a word known far beyond the shores of the United States of America. It is the first synonym that left-handers acknowledge as having no degrading implications. In fact, during the decades since its invention, the word *southpaw* has actually come to imply some advantageous qualities.

A *switch-hitter* is not necessarily a left-handed baseball player: he is a player who can bat with either hand. But even though the term isn't used exclusively to describe a lefty, it does seem worth explaining here. Many lefties, because they have to live in a right-handed world, learn to use their right hands as well as their left. Many so-called right-handed people were actually born lefties, then forced by their parents and teachers to switch and to learn how to write with their right hand. They

can still bat well with their left hands, however. Since left-handedness is considered to be an advantage in sports such as baseball, this is one activity in which born lefties are allowed to use their basic, natural preference for the left hand without criticism from spectators.

"Southpaw."

A "switch-hitter" isn't necessarily a lefty.

Left-handedness proved to be an advantage to a certain clan of Scots, who won many fights and gave us another curious word for lefties. Left-handedness tends to be inherited, but an unusually large number of this clan was born southpawed. One theory is that even this family's name, Kerr, was derived from the fact that so many of them were left-handed (*keir* or *caer* means "left" in Gaelic). They lived, from the 1500s on, in the turbulent Middle March or borderland between Scotland and England, where they were known as energetic "reivers" (marauders or plunderers, in short) and as good fighters.

As the Kerrs prospered and their clan grew, in the area around East Teviotdale, Liddesdale, Cessford and Ferniehurst, their sons and grandsons built new (fortified) homes. Because times of peace were rare in the Anglo-Scottish borderlands, a common type of building there was a peel tower—a stone fort, with storage areas on its lowest level, living quarters up above approached by a narrow, curving staircase.

Now, here's the crucial part of this story. The spiral staircase of the tower usually curved *clockwise*, so that a defender (on the higher part of the steps) held his unguarded left side against the wall and had his sword arm on the outside, free for action. His attacker, coming up the stairs, was at a disadvantage (unless he was left-handed!), because his sword arm was cramped against the curving wall to his right. The lefty Kerrs made good attackers. When it came to the business of protecting their own homes, they thought up an ingenious strategy: they built their staircases *counterclockwise*. Any right-handed attacker of a Kerr castle, it's true, would no longer be hampered by the curve . . . but the southpaw Kerr, poised above him on the steps, would be in a stronger position, with his right side partially protected by the inner wall and his sword-wielding left arm free for fighting. To this day, *corrie-fisted* (adapted over the centuries from "Kerr-handed" or "Kerr-fisted") is a synonym for southpaw—and a tribute to the strength and resourcefulness of this lefty clan.

A right-handed swordsman, defending his castle, has a slight advantage when fighting a right-handed attacker on a clockwise spiral staircase.

A left-handed defender is more vulnerable, and his sword arm is cramped for space on a conventional staircase.

Turn the steps around, so that they spiral up counterclockwise—then left-handed defenders like the canny Kerrs stand more than a fighting chance.

Words and their hidden meanings are the topic of this chapter. So we must not overlook one final example of linguistic prejudice: the often-derogatory implications of the terms *Left* and *Leftist* in politics.

The terms date back to the French Revolution, which broke out in 1789. At that time, the presiding officer of the French Assembly sat facing the moderates; the conservatives sat in a group on his right, and the radical revolutionary faction was seated to his left. Hence, *Leftists* were radicals, *Rightists* were conservatives. The terms stuck, and were transferred to other countries and other political struggles. After the Russian Revolution of 1917, the popular press began calling the Communist Party and its sympathizers *Leftists*. In the 1930s, a *Leftist* was generally understood to mean a Communist, in the United States and elsewhere. In 1935, the American playwright Clifford Odets played on words as he named his characters in the political drama "Waiting for Lefty," a play about the impoverished working classes. The character of Fatt represented capitalism; Lefty, the character who never appeared on stage, symbolized Communism.

Throughout the McCarthy era of the 1940s and 1950s, in the United States the adjective *leftist* was intended to mean Communist in the most derogatory sense. Then, through the 1960s and 1970s, as American radicals became slightly more conservative and the conservatives became slightly less rigid, a new term came into popular usage: *liberal*. *Left-*

A French Leftist in the 1780s.

A Russian Leftist, 1917.

American Leftist, suspect in the 1930s.

A 1970s "left-winger."

wing and *right-wing* now connote the extremist views at each end of the American political spectrum.

Let's watch the words we use. Should we all resolve to keep the words *left* and *right*, with all their innuendos, out of our conversations? If you are a liberal or a conservative, don't let people call you a *leftist* or a *rightist* instead. If you are a lefty, object if you are nicknamed a *cack-hander* or a *molly-dooker*.

And if some officious etymologist at a cocktail party tells you that in Hebrew the Biblical name Benjamin means *Son of the Right Hand*, connoting a worthy, helpful offspring, tell him that one of the most famous Benjamins of all time, the American scientist-publisher-inventor-writer-diplomat Benjamin Franklin, was a lefty.

Did you know...

... these famous lefties?

F. Lee Bailey
Sir James M. Barrie
Carmen Basilio
Robert Blake
The Boston Strangler
Lenny Bruce
McGeorge Bundy

C. P. E. Bach

The left is generally assumed to be the weaker hand.

Stone Age people were
ambidexterous, experts guess.

*In ancient China, the right
or female principle (yin)
complemented the yang,
the left and male force.
No favoritism toward
the right existed.*

*Bronze Age hunters
perfected the use
of one hand
—usually the right.*

A few Pharaohs were lefties.

*Even though
Julius Caesar
was a lefty,
the Romans became
one of the
most fanatically
pro-right groups
in history.*

24

A History of Left-Handedness

Witches and bastards, treacherous enemies and unfaithful husbands, clumsy characters who are gauche and sinister . . . all these were introduced in the first chapter. Are these the people who play a leading role in the history of left-handedness?

Not entirely, no. But the history of the left-handed is not a happy one, over the centuries, nor is it easy to document. Much is speculation. Going back to the beginning of human history, we find no written documents to tell us whether prehistoric men and women were predominantly left- or right-handed. Other evidence—tools, bones, cave drawings—has in fact led experts to guess that Stone Age man was ambidexterous.

During the Bronze Age, primitive people apparently began to show a preference for using their right hands. This was the period when bronze tools and weapons were forged from an alloy of copper and tin. The weapons were particularly important. One theory is that split-second timing became crucial for hunters using the new metal weapons: it was faster, perhaps, to perfect the use of one hand, rather than to take chances that the human brain might need a second or two to decide which hand was easier to use.

A spear held in the right hand of a Bronze Age warrior was more easily aimed to hit the heart of his opponent—or so goes another theory. Moreover, when fighters held shields in their left hands to protect their hearts (which they believed were on the left side of the body), only the right hand was free for spear-throwing or for wielding an axe.

Here's another explanation for the predominant right-handedness of our Bronze Age ancestors. Metal tools and weapons were difficult and time-consuming to make, and so they were handed down from parent to child for generations. Naturally, if the implement was shaped to be used by one hand rather than the other, the hand preference of the original owner would be passed down to the descendants, too. Yet another reason for the fact that Bronze Age righties outnumbered the left-handed may be the simple one of social pressure: were Bronze Age people any different from us in wanting to conform to their peer group? Whatever the explanation, an estimated 70% to 90% of these primitive people favored the right hand, while only 10% to 30% were lefties.

And so, around 2500 B.C., the favoring of the right began. The ancient Egyptians, founders of the oldest of empires, were predominantly right-handed (although a few of the Pharoahs, including Rameses II and Thothmes III, are believed to have been lefties). Their art records some lefties: Sardinian invaders, fierce raiders who sailed south across the Mediterranean sea, are depicted brandishing swords in their left hands and wearing shields on their right.

Egypt is in the northeastern part of the African continent. Elsewhere in Africa, among more primitive peoples, the right hand does not seem to have been so clearly predominant: a 50-50 split between lefties and righties is an estimate given for the Hottentots of southern Africa and their cousins the Bantus and nomadic Bushmen, as well as the Pygmies. In the Pacific area, the people of New Guinea and the Australian aborigines are believed to be similarly divided between right-handers and lefties.

Is it true, then, that "civilization" —particularly the use of relatively sophisticated tools and weapons— favors the development of one hand over the other, and that that predominant hand tends to be the right? It's a good argument. But the facts don't necessarily support it.

In the fourth century B.C., lefty Alexander the Great conquered most of the known world, and

The Ancient Egyptians, founders of the oldest empires, were predominantly right-handed.

Alexander the Great, left-handed conqueror of the world, reportedly found a whole nation of lefties.

American Indian cradleboards used to immobilize the baby's left arm.

reportedly he found a whole tribe of people who were all left-handed. In ancient China, highly civilized for a millenium before Alexander's conquests to its west, no favoritism toward the right existed. The right side was regarded as female (the *yin*), while the left side was male (the *yang* force or principle). Neither side was predominant. They were complimentary: *yin* and *yang* alternated for complete harmony. And that, of course, is as things should be.

But it's not the way things were or are today in most cultures of the world.

The Maori people of the Polynesian and Melanesian islands in the South Pacific, like the ancient Chinese, separated all things into male and female objects and attributes. The male was good, the female principle bad. And—you've guessed it—the good, male principle was associated with the right, the female with the left. Maori women weaving ceremonial cloths were forced to use their right hands and to weave from left to right in a right-handed direction. On the Indonesian islands off southeastern Asia, a child who showed a left-handed preference had the left hand tied to his or her left side. The Kaffirs of South Africa were once known for burying a left-handed child's hand in the burning sand of the desert.

On the North American continent, native Indian tribes once used less cruel but similarly forceful methods to make their children right-handed. A baby was customarily strapped to

Did you know...

. . . these famous lefties?

Charlie Chaplin
Ted Williams
Gentleman Jim Corbett
Henry Wallace
Rod Laver
Olivia De Havilland
Gov. Brendan T. Byrne

Judy Garland

a cradleboard and carried on the mother's back. As the baby grew, the right arm was freed but the left remained strapped to the board. Thus virtually every Indian child grew up to be a righty. When the use of the traditional cradleboard was abandoned, the percentage of lefties among the North American Indians, not surprisingly, dramatically increased.

Among the Hebrew, Greek and Roman peoples from whom other North Americans and Europeans derive much of their culture, the right hand was generally the winner. Most of the Hebrews were right-handed. But the Old Testament of the Bible relates several good stories about the left-handed minority. Best known are the tales about the

Benjaminites (ironically, their name means "sons of the right hand"). When the Benjaminites fought the Israelites, being outnumbered 26,000 to 400,000, they cleverly deployed "700 chosen men left-handed." According to the story in the Book of Judges, every one of these 700 "could sling stones at hair breadth and not miss." Later in Biblical history, as recorded in the Book of Chronicles, an army of lefties came to the aid of King David: they were described as "armed with bows" they could use ambidexterously, for "they could use both the right and left in hurling stones and shooting arrows."

Ehud is the most noted southpaw whose story is dramatically told in the Bible, in the Book of Judges. Ehud was chosen by God to deliver his people from the bondage of the King of Moab. He concealed a dagger, strapped to his right thigh, under his clothes. Before his audience with the King, presumably he was searched: but the right-handed guards who frisked him ran their hands over his left thigh, where a righty would naturally place a concealed knife. Ehud was able to surprise the King and stab him, then lead his people to freedom.

The Greeks, too, favored the right hand, although they were not bigoted about their preference. Their great philosopher, Plato, believed that ambidexterity was natural. "Though our limbs are by nature balanced," he wrote, "we create a difference in them by bad habit." He argued that in certain pursuits—especially in fighting and in contact sports—men should be trained to use both hands with equal strength.

Plato's belief was that it was only "the stupidity of nurses and mothers" that made us "all one-armed." His theory was that right-handed mothers or nurses carried babies in their left arms, so that their right hands were free for work: their children became lefties. Vice versa, left-handed women brought up right-handed children. If this were true, purely left-handed generations would follow right-handed generations in alternating sequence. And there never seems to have been a time when one hand was 100%

Right-handed mothers keep their right hands free for work, carry on their left arms babies who will become lefties. That's what Plato said.

dominant in a single generation.

Aristotle corrected Plato's teachings by asserting that our arms are not naturally equally balanced. The Greek philosophers, however, did much to promote ambidexterity. The Greeks even applied their separate-but-equal principles to their writing. They borrowed the Phoenicians' alphabet and their style of writing from right to left, then incorporated it into their own (left-to-right) system of writing, thus inventing *boustrophedon*, the ancient Greek writing in which lines run alternately right-to-left and left-to-right. *Boustrophedon* means, literally, "turning as the ox turns (while plowing)," and the lines of the writing resemble the furrows plowed back and forth across the fields of ancient Greece.

The ancient Romans, like the Greeks, believed that the right was the lucky side. In spite of the fact that Julius Caesar and the Emperor Tiberius were lefties, the Romans carried their preference to extremes and became one of the most pro-right groups in history. They fought with the right hand, adopted the

Great lefties of the Middle Ages included Charlemagne of France, crowned Holy Roman Emperor in 800 A.D.

right-handed salute and handshake, and standardized writing from left to right. They subtly tried to stamp out left-handedness.

During the Middle Ages in Europe, little was done to help the plight of the left-hander. The most important nobleman at court sat on the King's right: hence the term, "right-hand man." Great lefties included Charlemagne, King of the Franks, who journeyed to Rome to save the Pope from invaders and was crowned Holy Roman Emperor in the year 800. Lefties might be heroes . . . but

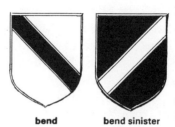

bend   bend sinister

The bend sinister or left-handed stripe across a coat of arms was the mark of a bastard—such as William the Conqueror.

if they were sons "of the left hand," bastard children, the coat of arms on their shield was marked with the *bend sinister*—a band passing across the shield from the upper corner on the bearer's left down to the lower corner on his right. This was the mirror image or opposite direction of the normal ornamental band used in heraldry. William the Conqueror, who subdued England and became its king in 1066, was one military leader who proudly carried the bastard's left-striped coat of arms into battle.

When armies of Crusaders traveled to the Holy Land in the eleventh, twelfth and thirteenth centuries, they went to do battle with the followers of the prophet Mohammed. The Moslems hold the dubious distinction of being the most pro-right group in history, outdoing the medieval Christians and even the Romans in their disdain for the left. The Moslems' prejudice had a practical reason. Water is scarce in the desert, and washing was difficult, centuries ago. Since the Arabs ate from a communal bowl with their right hand, the left hand—reserved for cleaning themselves in matters of particularly personal hygiene—became "unclean." Even touching another person with the left hand implied a social insult. The worst fate that could befall a Moslem in the old days was the loss of the right hand—brutal punishment for thieves, who were thereby excommunicated psychologically as well as physically from their society. Although the ritual of communal eating gradually disappeared, the disdain for the "unclean" left hand was retained in Moslem countries, while the right hand was honored. This cultural attitude was transmitted to the invading Christian Europeans, who were already prejudiced against the left.

The Industrial Revolution of 18th- and 19th-century Europe, more than five hundred years later, did not do much good for the lefties. Just like the hand-made tools and weapons of the Bronze Age, so machine-made tools of modern industry were designed for righties.

The history of left-handedness took a turn for the better in the land traditionally associated with freedom

Christian Crusaders traveled to the Holy Land to battle the Moslems, the most anti-left group in history. Then they brought some of the Arabic prejudices home.

Machines of the Industrial Revolution were designed for righties.

and opportunity, the United States of America. The concept that an American should be judged for personal qualities alone, not for social position or family, was applied to hand preference. In a country of booming expansion and the hard work that led to prosperity, there was, besides, little time for discrimination against the left-handed. In rural areas, the children of farming and ranching families received little pressure from their parents or teachers to use their right hands—so long as they got their chores done.

In the public and church-run schools of America's towns and cities, however, teachers encouraged students to write with their right hands: many are the stories of staunch lefties who had their knuckles rapped, or worse. But at the turn of this century, Americans began to do research on the education of the left-handed. Enlightened parents saw to it that their children were not forced to switch. The author Jessamyn West, born in Indiana in 1902, had such parents. She has related that she went to school "in the days when teachers did not allow left-handed penmanship—even to the extent of tying the left arms of students behind their backs, until they learned to write 'correctly.' " West's parents came to her rescue. "My mother sent me to school with a note saying, 'God intended this child to use her left hand,' " she has recalled. "So the teacher let me alone. I don't think she was afraid to go against my mother, but she wasn't going to go against God."

American newspapers and magazines began in this century to disseminate information on the psychological and physical effects of forcing left-handed children to switch from their natural preference. Progressive parents let their children alone. Social prejudices against lefties changed. In sports—a big business in the U.S. since the turn of the century—left-handedness was seen as an asset. Most experts agree that the United States is the first country in which hand preference has, in general, been allowed to develop as it would. In the land of "live and let live," left-handedness may not be exactly flourishing, but at least it has been allowed to grow.

So how many lefties are there now, in the United States and other countries of the world? It's difficult to say. First of all, left-handedness is not totally simple to define. Among people who are not right-handed are included strong left-handers (all-the-way lefties), part-time left-handers (who may write and eat with their left hand, but do other things with their right), and ambidexterous folk (who use either hand with equal skill—or equal clumsiness). The most important question seems to be: which hand is used for *skilled* tasks, such as writing, eating, working?

Statistics on left-handedness seem to rely on the hand used for writing as the chief criterion. But we will never know how many people were born to be strong lefties, but were forced to learn how to write with their right hand. So the numbers

In Taiwan and the People's Republic of China, pressures have resulted in almost no left-handed writers.

In booming 19th-century America, the general attitude toward lefties (and everyone else) was "Live and let live—just get the work done."

vary. What's the percentage of left-handed people in the world? Four per cent? Seven percent? Eight-and-a-half percent? Even thirty percent? There are dozens of estimates based on dozens of samplings.

One study worth mentioning was conducted with school children in Michigan, back in 1947. This study is important for two reasons. First, the sample was large: over 225,000 people were involved. Second, the results seemed to show the effect of social pressure on lefties: in the first year of school, over ten percent of the children were left-handed, but by their twelfth year of school 3½% had switched to the right, so that only 6½% remained as lefties.

More recent American studies place the percentage of left-handers in the United States at between fifteen and twenty percent. Naturally, in countries where the southpaw is still disdained, that percentage shrinks.

In modern China, for example, there is great discrimination against left-handers. The Chinese people who live on Taiwan seem to have almost completely eliminated the use of the left hand in writing. Social pressure seems to be the reason for the curious difference in the writing habits of Chinese people living on that island and those living in California. Researchers doing a comparative study found that, among 4148 subjects on Taiwan, "a scant 0.7 percent used the left hand for writing, and 1.5 percent used the left hand for eating." But in California, among 538 people of

Did you know...

... that lefties are three times more likely than right-handers to drink too much? A lefty's frustrations at adjusting to a right-handed world took the blame for this, for years. But new research shows the right hemisphere of the brain has a lower tolerance than the left for alcohol, rendering lefties much more susceptible.

Chinese descent, 6.5 percent used their left hands for writing (while 9.9 percent of a non-Oriental group of 7146 Californians wrote with their left hands).

The interesting result of this study is that the Chinese people on Taiwan, when tested for hand preference in activities *not* subjected to strong social pressure (throwing a ball or hammering a nail, for example), showed very nearly the same degree of left-handedness or right-handedness as people subjected to similar tests in the United States of America. Also, the left-handed Taiwanese people, who had frequently been requested or forced to switch from left to right in writing and eating, tended to use their right hands *less*

frequently for *other* tasks than people who had not been subjected to such strong social pressure. When suppressed in a critical area, left-handedness apparently asserts itself stubbornly in others.

In mainland China, the social pressure on lefties to switch to the right has political pressure behind it, too. The Communist government of the People's Republic of China has decided—in the interests of organization and uniformity—that there are no left-handed people among the 800 million Chinese (just as there are no homosexuals).

Nearby Japan has a different form of government, but its society still shows the effects of centuries of discrimination against the left-handed. People who were born left-handed once had to hide that fact: left-handed students were beaten, a left-handed girl had no chance of finding a husband, and, if she revealed her secret after marriage, her husband could divorce her. A left-handed Japanese man once risked expulsion from his social, economic and political community.

After World War II, new generations of Japanese began to change old prejudices. Japan now has organizations for southpaws to join, products for lefties to buy and campaigns meant to erase the stigma against left-handedness. One big help to lefties in Japan has been the popularity of baseball—a sport in which the southpaw has a clear advantage. A few years ago, a record on Japan's top ten hits was a song called "My Boyfriend is a Lefty."

We have evidence, then, that prejudices dating back centuries can be changed, and that left-handed people can be allowed to develop their own full potential. How many left-handed people would inhabit our world if ideal conditions prevailed? To quote Dr. Bryng Bryngelson, speech pathologist, former head of the Speech and Hearing Clinic at the University of Minnesota and a man who has been engaged in research on left-handedness for over thirty years: "If there were no interference on the part of parents and teachers, 34 out of every 100 children born today would be left-handed, and about three percent would be using both hands with equal dexterity."

If there were no interference . . . yes. But the sad truth is that throughout history, for a few practical reasons and for many beliefs based on superstitious nonsense, right-handed people *have* interfered with the natural inclinations and abilities of lefties.

Some of these superstitions and beliefs will be explained in the next chapter.

Superstitions ...and a Yankee's Plea for Common Sense

Moving counterclockwise, "widdershins," was the method of witches and warlocks who defied the laws of God and Nature.

What's really behind all this preference for the right hand and strong prejudice against the left? Long-standing beliefs that date back to the beginning of human history.

Sun worship is probably the very oldest form of religion, and it has a great deal to do with our preference for the right. Imagine that you are facing the sun at mid-day: you are facing south, so the sun has risen on your left hand (in the east), and it will be traveling across the sky (or so it seems) until it sets in the west, on your right hand. The sun isn't moving at all, of course—it's the earth that is rotating. But it appears to you that the sun, the giver of life and warmth and food, is circling across the sky from your left to right,

35

in a clockwise direction. *Clockwise*, therefore, must be the "correct" or magically powerful way to turn. Primitive people believed this, and more sophisticated people have had faith in the principle for centuries.

The swastika—unhappy symbol, for us, of Adolf Hitler and the Nazis —is actually an ancient religious symbol of good luck and well-being. It dates back to Neolithic times, and for ancient Egyptians it was a symbol of the sun, used in ritual processions. Formed by what we call a "Greek" cross, with the ends of the arms bent at right angles, it is a representation of clockwise movement . . . or, if the ends of the arms are reversed, of motion in a counterclockwise direction. Its name comes from the Sanskrit word *svasti*, meaning good fortune. North American Indians, as well as people in Asia and the other parts of the Old World, used the swastika symbol. If you stand facing north, of course, the sun seems to rotate in a *counterclockwise* direction, from your right hand to your left. In some societies, therefore, the reversed or counterclockwise swastika (also called a *suavastika*) became the symbol of good luck. This was true in southern India, for example, and there is evidence that the left-handed swastika was used in prehistoric Britain.

The ancient Greek augurs or soothsayers were among the priests who faced north as they went through rituals of slaughtering an animal and prophesying the future by examining its entrails. The sun rose on the augurs' right—hence

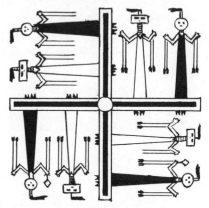

> The swastika, ancient symbol of the sun's rotation, was a good-luck symbol world-wide until the 1930s.

A Navaho Indian counterclockwise swastika, with the gods of mountains, rivers and rain.

Early Germanic rune of the Wolf's Cross is related to the once-benevolent swastika.

Nordic rune, symbol of the Vehmic courts of medieval Germany.

Nazi swastika of the 1930s.

lucky—side. The conquering Romans adopted many of the Greeks' religious and superstitious beliefs and the left became for them, too, the unpropitious side. Later European Christians picked up the belief. But the idea that the right hand and clockwise movement toward it are "lucky" or "good" and "natural" was shared by other groups as far apart as Africa and South America, as different as the Buddhists of China, the Moslems of Arabia, and the Hindu Brahmins. Even the whirling dervishes of the Islamic world spun clockwise, from left to right, in the "natural" direction of the sun as they saw it.

Whirling dervishes of the Moslem world spun clockwise, from left to right, in what they believed was the natural direction of the sun.

A few superstitions and cultures favored the left. Egyptians thought it was lucky to enter a house left foot first—especially if the building was haunted. The Incas of ancient Peru considered left-handedness a sign of good fortune. One of their beloved chiefs was called Lloque Yupanqui, a name meaning Left-Handed. Aztecs in early Mexico believed that you must use the left hand when taking medicine to aid your kidneys—the right hand when curing the liver. On the same continent, in what is today the southwestern United States, Zuni Indians were also pro-left, believing that the left hand was the older and wiser of the two.

Almost all other societies—ancient and modern, American, African or Eastern—have systems of beliefs that favor the right. Before European "civilization" reached the New World, in pre-Columbian South America, the Mayan Indians had a curious ritual to foretell the future. A soothsayer would vigorously rub both his legs and—you may have guessed it—if the right leg twitched, the future was bright. If the muscles of the left leg began twitching, impending doom was foretold.

North American Indian sign language also showed bias for the right. The right hand raised meant "brave," "powerful" and "good." But the left hand placed over the right connoted "death," "burial."

In Africa, the Meru people of Kenya believe that the left hand of their *mugwe* or holy man has such sinister power that he must

Aztecs in early Mexico used the left hand for medicine for kidney trouble, the right when curing the liver.

Mayan Indians were pro-right: the twitching of a soothsayer's left leg foretold disaster.

The Incas of ancient Peru considered left-handedness a sign of good fortune.

"Let not thy left hand know what thy right doeth," says the Bible. (Often quoted out of context, this is actually advice on the modest way to give money to the poor.) Engraving by lefty Albrecht Dürer.

On the final Day of Judgment, God blesses the saved on His right hand; on His left, sinners are cast out.

Joan of Arc, burned as a heretic and witch, was drawn in contemporary sketches as a lefty—perhaps just because she was in league with the Devil.

keep it hidden. Hindus use only their right hand to touch themselves above the waist, while below the waist the left hand is used exclusively, a habit that seems to be a reflection of Moslem custom.

In the Judaic and Christian lore influencing much of Europe and the Americas, the Old and New Testaments of the Bible are the source for many strong beliefs and traditions that lead to a preference for the right over the left. "If I forget thee, O Jerusalem," sings the author of the 137th Psalm, "let my right hand forget her cunning." Jesus Christ, during His Sermon on the Mount, told His presumably right-handed followers how to donate alms: "Let not thy left hand know what they right hand doeth." Christ traditionally sits at the right hand of God the Father. And, on the final Day of Judgment, God blesses on His right hand those people who are saved and will inherit His kingdom; on His left hand, sinners are cast out.

This Biblical tradition led to many superstitions that did nothing to make the lefthander's life easier during the Middle Ages. Those who preferred left to right, or counter-clockwise movement to clockwise motion, were sometimes considered in league with the Devil. Joan of Arc, burned at the stake in 1431 for being a heretic and witch, has been depicted in many portraits as being left-handed (but it is uncertain whether she really was a lefty or whether she is the victim of medieval propaganda in this sense, too). Hundreds of superstitions dating back to the Middle Ages link the left hand and left-handedness to evil and bad luck.

Benjamin Franklin, statesman of the 18th century, a scientist who trained himself to use his left hand as well as his right, tried to persuade his fellow Americans to abandon their superstitious nonsense about the left hand. Tackling a serious subject with a light touch, he penned one of the first pleas for rational understanding and compassion toward lefties.

"I address myself to all friends of youth, and conjure them to direct their compassionate regard to my unhappy fate, in order to remove the prejudices of which I am a victim," he wrote in his *Petition to Those Who Have the Superintendency of Education.* He wrote as if he were his own left hand, and referred to his right hand—the hand that had always been favored by his teachers— as his "sister," as he humorously pleaded for a more tolerant and rational attitude toward natural lefties.

In spite of Ben Franklin's persuasiveness and the writings of all other rational thinkers since Plato, pleas that equal attention and respect should be given to both hands and arguments that ambidexterity is an extraordinarily useful skill have not yet won over most of the people in the world.

"From my infancy, I have been led to consider my sister as being of a more educated rank," wrote Ben. "I was suffered to grow up without the least instruction, while nothing was spared in her education. She had masters to teach her writing, drawing, music and other accomplishments, but if by chance I touched a pencil, a pen, or a needle I was bitterly rebuked; and more than once I have been beaten for being awkward, and wanting a graceful manner. It is true, my sister associated with me upon some occasions; but she always made a point of taking the lead, calling upon me only from necessity, or to figure by her side."

"But conceive not, sirs," Ben continued, "that my complaints are instigated merely by vanity. No; my uneasiness is occasioned by an object much more serious. It is the practice of our family, that the whole business of providing for its subsistence falls upon my sister and myself. If any indisposition should attack my sister—and I mention it in confidence, upon this occasion, that she is subject to the gout, the rheumatism, and cramp, without making mention of other accidents—what would be the fate of our poor family? Must not the regret of our parents be excessive, at having placed so great a difference between sisters who are so perfectly equal? Alas! We must perish from distress; for it would not be in my power even to scrawl a suppliant petition for relief, having been obliged to employ the hand of another in transcribing the request which I have now the honor to prefer to you.

"Condescend, sirs, to make my parents sensible of the injustice of an exclusive tenderness, and of the necessity of distributing their care and affection among all their children equally.

"I am, with profound respect, Sirs,
Your obedient servant,
THE LEFT HAND"

Benjamin Franklin,
a self-taught
left-handed writer
and scientist,
wittily begged his
fellow Americans to
abandon superstitious
prejudice against
the left hand.

"I address myself to all friends of
youth," Franklin wrote, asking
teachers to instruct lefties in using
"a pencil, a pen or a needle."

Ben signed both
the Declaration of
Independence and
the Constitution
with his left hand.

Did you know...

. . . these famous lefties?

George Burns
Louis Harris
Jack the Ripper
Reggie Jackson
Robert McNamara
Ben Hogan
Emperor Tiberius
Betty Grable

In our own society, many of the old superstitions hang on. For example, since Judas spilled salt at the Last Supper, this minor accident was and is believed to bring bad luck: to avoid ill fortune when you spill salt, you must throw a pinch of it over your left shoulder, to ward off the evil spirit lurking there.

We've all heard the one about getting out of bed left foot first—the cause of a bad day and a bad temper. But do you know these other superstitions about right and left?

If your right eye twitches . . . you'll see a friend. If your left eye twitches . . . you'll see an enemy.

A ringing in your right ear means that someone is praising you. A ringing in your left ear . . . someone is cursing or maligning you.

If you have an itchy right palm . . . you'll receive money. If you have an itchy left palm . . . you'll lose money or owe someone a debt.

Lefties with sensitive left palms, take heart! German folklore reverses the last superstition: the Germans believe that cash is coming when your *left* palm itches. So have faith, and read on, in the next chapter, about many other little-known advantages that lefties really hold over the righties in this world.

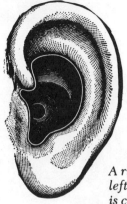

A ringing in your left ear means someone is cursing you.

If your right eye twitches, you'll see a friend.

If your left eye twitches, you'll see an enemy.

Unexpected Advantages of Being Left-Handed

Well, you've just read a lot of words about the plight of being a lefty in a right-handed world. And if you yourself are a southpaw, it's likely that you not only were aware of these problems but could add a few of your own grievances to the list, too.

The question must arise: is there *any* advantage to being left-handed? The answer is: *YES*, definitely.

Some machines and gadgets do exist that are *not* geared for the right-handed. One of these is an office machine more than a century old: the typewriter, which has its most frequently-used keys divided, fairly, between the two hands.

British cars are another example. People in Britain—and a very few other countries—still drive on the left-hand side of the highway, so the steering wheel is on the right side of the car and the gear shift (perfect for lefties) is on the driver's left. In the United States and other drive-to-the-right nations, toll booths on turnpikes, bridges and tunnels are always on the driver's left (but is that really an advantage?).

The most important advantage for lefties is not that some machines are built with a bias in favor of the left hand. The real, secret, advantage is that left-handed people are forced to learn to use their right hands, too; therefore they are likely to be reasonably ambidexterous. If an accident puts their dominant hand out of action, they can usually manage with their right hand to do most necessary tasks (but pity the poor righty in the same situation).

Having been forced to adapt, more or less, to a right-handed world gives a lefty other advantages. One study done at Boston University showed that left-handers are more emotionally independent, more determined, and more apt to have an "I'm my own person" attitude to life than the typical righty. Lefties prefer to figure out problems for themselves, this study seems to show, while righties have a greater tendency to believe what other people tell them. It's easy to figure the reasons for this: southpaws encounter so many challenges to their competence and autonomy that they are almost bound to wind up with these attitudes.

One psychologist, Theodore Blau, has speculated on the process that teaches the lefty to be a different kind of person from the typical righty. "I suspect that it's not one experience, but a long series of experiences, through which the left-handed person begins to learn, very early in life, that the word 'right' has a double meaning," he has said. "It has a positional meaning, and it has a moral meaning." As the left-handed child grows up, the after-effects of this early learning persist, he speculates. "Later on in life," Blau says, "this stubborness may become forthrightness or a willingness to 'go it alone' in spite of other people's objections."

Lefties have a distinct advantage in certain sports such as baseball, tennis and boxing. This we all know.

But what about the lefty who enjoys sports as a pure amateur? There are many activities in which left-handedness seems to be an asset. They are as diverse as underwater diving . . . and art and architecture. Can you guess what these three pursuits have in common? They all require acute visual perception—and left-handers are believed to have greater spatial competence than righties.

Two studies at the University of Cincinnati have shown that left-handers have an unusually good sense of distance and proportion. The people tested were professional architects and students of architecture. The test results showed, first,

Lefties are more independent, more determined, and more likely to figure out problems instead of believing what other people tell them.

that "both groups tend to be more left-handed than would be normally expected," and, secondly, that "all the left-handed students followed complex directions about drawing a spatial maze (an architectural exercise) perfectly, whereas over 50% of the right-handed students erred."

Another group of researchers has reported that lefties make unusually good underwater divers because they adapt better than righties to visual distortion. Lefties have this advantage because they use receptors on *both* sides of their brain to discriminate and adjust to what they are seeing underwater.

Most of the advantages of being left-handed are directly related to brain organization—which in left-handers tends to be less specialized or more diffuse than in the brains of righties. Regarded for years as a disadvantage, this difference has recently come to be recognized as an advantage, because it makes left-handers adaptable.

Southpaws have an advantage as musicians, for example, because they and ambidexterous people have unusually good musical memories. The storage and retrieval of the sound of musical pitches happens in two places, in the right as well as the left hemisphere of their brain—this is the theory resulting from tests done at the University of California in San Diego.

Jerre Levy, a psychologist doing research in brain organization and handwriting, supports the belief that lefties are inclined to use both halves of the brain more equitably than righties. "What this means is that most left-handers probably tend to recover faster from results of brain damage, such as loss of speech due to a stroke," she has speculated.

We all — left-handed or right-handed or ambidexterous—use both halves of our brain, of course. Lefties just do this a little more than the rest of us, if recent research is correct. Right-handed people make *more* use of brain cells in the left hemisphere, however, while six out of ten lefties use their hands and brain in "inverted" style—they cross over and employ the right half of the brain more fully (even though they do not give up use of the left hemisphere). Guess what? The left half of the brain is known to control most of the functions concerned with speech and with linear thought . . . while the right half of the brain (the side most used by lefties) is the hemisphere that is free to dream and imagine. Lefties may be more creative than other mortals.

Meditation and certain drugs have been used by researchers and others in an attempt to get in touch with this creative right half of the brain. In recent years, programs and courses have been devised to help people to exercise this aspect of themselves and to develop their creativity.

Lefty . . . because you use the right half of your brain every day . . . you have a head start! And you are being recognized, at last, as someone who is not just "different," but as a person with unusual and innate different potential.

PRINCE CHARLES • CAROL BURNETT • JIMMY CONNORS • WALTER SCHIRRA

The Science of the Left

HARRY TRUMAN • MARILYN MONROE • PABLO PICASSO • BOB DYLAN

Mammals have tusks that may spiral counterclockwise or clockwise. (The Wallachian sheep).

A helix, a spiral curving in either direction, is Nature's simplest expression of preference for left or right.

A flounder is a flatfish that swims on its side. As the fish matures, the eye that consistently faces the ocean floor slowly moves around to join the eye on the upper side—left or right, according to species.

A molecule of DNA (carrier of hereditary characteristics) is a chain of two strands of chemicals, twisted into a double helix.

Left in the Natural World

People, as we know, have strong preferences for right or left, for clockwise versus counterclockwise movement. Is this true in the rest of the natural world? The answer is *yes:* animals and plants, even minerals, show clear preferences for the left or for the right in terms of growth and motion.

"Hand" preference in nature—since rocks, plants and animals do not possess hands—expresses itself most basically in terms of the helix, a spiral curve through a cylindrical or conical shape. The helix may turn to the right, in a clockwise direction, or to the left, counterclockwise. The news is that Mother Nature isn't biased.

Quartz, for example, is the most common rock-forming mineral in the earth's crust. Sandstone is made of it; it is the major component of granite; with the addition of minute amounts of other elements, which change its color, quartz crystals become the semi-precious stones we call amethyst, citrine, cairngorm, rock crystal and rose quartz; in non-crystalline form, quartz can be agate, chalcedony, jasper, bloodstone, sardonyx, opal and flint. It's everywhere! So? The interesting fact, for us, is that its chains of atoms may be linked in either a left-turning or a right-turning helix.

Left-turning and right-turning helixes occur in the major building blocks of organic matter, as well as in inanimate materials. Amino acids, for example, the essential components of proteins, are invariably *left*-spiraled in living tissue. In short, life on this planet has been structured with the left preference as an integral part of the master plan.

Apart from the satisfying knowledge that all is not "right" in the natural world around us, do we humans derive any practical benefit from our information about this left and right spiraling which is visible only through a microscope?

Yes, in several instances. Table sugar (dextrose) is right-spiraled. Fructose, occurring in honey and many fruits, is different from dextrose only in that it spirals to the left . . . but research has shown that it seems sweeter. You can use less fructose and still enjoy the same taste of sweetness. This is an obvious advantage for people who wish to reduce their consumption of sugar. And it's a good example of *left* being *better.*

Medicine has progressed because of our knowledge of left and right helixes. Take the example of thyroxin, a hormone produced naturally by the thyroid gland to regulate metabolism. Thyroxin is given to patients who need to reduce the cholesterol in their blood: however, thyroxin can cause nervousness and weight loss. A synthetic form of thyroxin, with the helix turning in the opposite direction, reportedly achieves the same good results as the natural hormone—but without undesirable side effects. Adrenalin, according to reports of medical researchers, is twelve times more efficient at constricting blood vessels when it spirals to the left then when it is right-turning.

Smokers take note: even nicotine, currently the object of research, has a left and a right spiraled form. In tobacco, nicotine is formed in a left helix (and here it is named levonicotine from *laevus*, Latin for "left"), and, as we all now know, it has toxic effects. But there is also a type of nicotine with a right helix: dextronicotine. It doesn't occur in tobacco, but it has been created in the laboratory, and its toxic effects are reported to be far less serious. Even though it will represent a triumph for the *right*, we can all hope that dextronicotine may solve a problem in public health.

Not all of Nature's helixes are so small that they can be seen only through a microscope. Many helixes can be seen every day with the naked eye—in the plant world, for example. Plant stems and stalks, even leaves, flowers and stems, may be formed in the pattern of these three-dimensional curves. Leaves may be attached to the stalk in a spiral that is a clockwise or counterclockwise helix.

In climbing plants such as vines, which may twist their way up a support in a clockwise or a sinistral approach, the helix pattern is impossible to overlook. The twining and trailing plants of the genus *Convolvulus* were even named for their convolutions or coils. Members of this genus (bindweed and morning-glory) attempt to climb in a right-handed fashion, and most twisting plants stick to a consistent system of climbing and coiling in the same direction as other members of their species. Honeysuckle, for example, appears to be consistently left-helixed. The spectacle of left-handed honeysuckle criss-crossing with right-handed bindweed, as they climb a common support, has inspired at least one recent song (by the British duo, Flanders and Swann) and

The fragrant honeysuckle vine always twists to the left as it climbs. As poets have noted, it often intertwines with right-handed bindweed.

directions. As in the plant world, members of one species usually all make their patterns in the same direction. But strange variations may happen. Occasionally a species will be left-handed in one part of the world, right-oriented in another geographic location. Sometimes a real individualist will grow its shell in a direction opposite to that of the other members of the family . . . making itself a highly desirable specimen for enthusiastic shell collectors and perhaps dooming itself to an early demise!

Large spirals of calcareous (limestone-like) material found in Wyoming and Nebraska puzzled geologists for years. These strange helixes, nicknamed "Devil's Corkscrews,"

poetic comment as long as four centuries ago, when the English dramatist Ben Jonson observed: "The blue bindweed doth itself enfold with honeysuckle."

Left-handed and right-handed spirals can be seen on the bark of beech trees and chestnuts, as well as on the trunks of many evergreens. These helixes seem to go either way, clockwise or counterclockwise, for no apparent reason. As we said before, Nature is not biased.

Helixes can be seen in the animal world, too—for example, in the beautiful coiled shells of mollusks such as snails. The coils may twist to the left or to the right. Even extinct mollusks, whose shells have been discovered by geologists, had shells with helixes turning in both

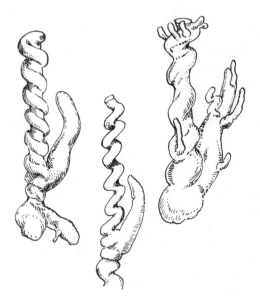

Geologists were puzzled for years by the sinistral and dextral spirals of the fossils known as the Devil's Corkscrews.

are six feet or more in length. Some spiral to the left, others to the right. At first experts thought they might be fossils of giant twining plants (they do contain fossilized roots). Then came a discovery: in this arid terrain lived a prehistoric rodent, *Palaeocastor*. In Miocene times, *Palaeocastor* constructed colonies of burrows, as prairie dogs do today. As the animals dug, they sometimes turned to the left, sometimes to the right, and as they passed through the narrow tunnels they gradually hardened their walls. This happened as long as 25 million years ago. Gradually, over hundreds of thousands of years, empty burrows filled with soil washed in by rain and with growing plants. Because of their hardened walls, the shape was preserved—and they became fossilized casts of the amazing Corkscrews.

Most crabs and lobsters have one claw that looks slightly larger than the other. The male fiddler crab takes this enlargement to the extreme—growing one enormous front claw which he seems to hold like a fiddle or violin. The large claw, which may be either the left or the right pincher, is part of his sexual appeal, but quite useless for food-gathering.

Some fish, as they grow, make the left-right choice in a way that is bizarre. Young flounder and sole, for example, look and behave just like most other fish; they have an eye, of course, on either side of their bodies. As these flatfish grow older, however, one eye begins to migrate across the body. (Human adolescents

Ammonite.

Agate-shell (Achatina mauritiana).

American pond-snails.

Snails and their prehistoric ancestors (fossils of extinct mollusks) have shells twisting to left or right. An occasional individualist will reverse the pattern of the species.

The chambered nautilus, a mollusk of the Pacific and Indian oceans, coils its shell as it builds (and moves into) a series of small, partitioned chambers.

think *they* have growing pains!) Ultimately both eyes are located side by side, on either the left or right half of the body, and the fish lives and swims with its "blind" side toward the sea bottom. Both eyes continue to operate independently. The fish within one species of the sole and flounder family are usually consistent in their choice of locating their eyes on the left or on the right. For example, turbot is an "eyes-left" flounder, while halibut, another flounder, keeps its eyes on the right. (Lefties may not have to be told that turbot is considered superior eating). Occasionally one individualistic fish will switch its eyes to the "wrong" side, opposite to that of the rest of its species.

Flounder and sole may suffer a troubled adolescence, but the genus of fish called anableps, which also has to make a choice between left and right as it grows up, could have a very difficult love life. Anableps lives in tidal fresh waters along the coast of Central and South America. It is one of the strangest fish in the world. For starters, it has four eyes (two lenses, each divided horizontally) so that it can see above and below the water simultaneously; every few seconds, the anableps has to duck its head under water, to keep the upper half of its eyes wet. It bears its young alive, instead of laying eggs. But its sexual capabilities are strictly one-sided. Fertilization takes place inside the female—and each female anableps has an opening on *either* her port *or* starboard side. The male

Male narwhals, small Arctic whales, grow their left tusks into counterclockwise spirals of ivory, as long as nine feet. Narwhals were hunted for these tusks when people believed in their magical properties.

anableps has a similar arrangement: he is either a lefty or a righty. Conjugation is possible only when one fish is a portsider and the other has developed on the starboard side. Sad indeed for the poor anableps that seeks the attention of a similar-sided mate! Luckily for the species, the mix between lefties and righties is about even.

The narwhal is another sea creature with its own twist in the left-right story. Living in polar waters, the narwhal is a small whale, about twelve feet in length. The male has two tusks—one of which is an ivory spiral several feet long (usually more than half the body length), certainly the longest tooth in the world by any standards. The left tusk is normally the one that grows to this extraordinary length, and its coil is also to the left. On the rare occasions when both teeth extend, both form a left-turning helix. Why this clear preference for the left, and why a tusk that spirals counterclockwise as it grows? The cause may be the interaction of the animal's slight rotation as it swims and a slight stress on the tusk as it is growing. Exactly how this "sea unicorn" uses its long tooth is unclear: its exclusive occurrence in males suggest that it is part of the animal's sexual display or a weapon used in sexually-motivated combat with other males.

The sex life of birds offers another

strange example of Nature's occasional preference for the left. In young female birds, ovaries and oviducts on the left and right sides are developed to the same degree. As the birds mature, however, the right ovaries and oviducts degenerate; the left set enlarges greatly, taking on all the functions of reproduction and egg-laying. Birds favor the left in another way: in canaries and finches, the brain center for song is clearly in the left hemisphere (just as a human being's speech center is usually located on that side).

At least one type of bird makes left-right choices in the way it grows its beak. The crossbill is a small finch-like bird. As its name implies, its beak or bill has long, curved mandibles with narrow tips crossed almost like the blades of scissors. The bill is designed for pulling seeds from cones, and the bird uses it much as we would use a pair of pliers. The species of crossbill prevalent in North America has the upper mandible closing to the left, while the common European species has a bill which closes to the right. And who can say why?

Some answers to questions about left-right preferences in the natural world have been found in the research laboratory. Mice and rats in particular have been scrutinized in the laboratory for "paw preference."

Mice and rats consistently seem to use one paw in preference to the other when they are eating, so they clearly can be divided into lefties and righties. Left-pawed mice are not a minority group, however: they make up about fifty percent of the mouse population. The 50-50 natural balance cannot be changed. Selective breeding of mice for left-paw preference resulted in no significant change after three generations. Similar results—no more and no fewer lefties—were reported after selective breeding of eight generations of rats. Nature is even-handed here. So, in another sense, are most of the mice: even though they exhibit clear paw preference, most of them will simply use the "easy" paw when confronted with a feeding tube specially designed to make eating with one paw more awkward than with the other. Only a stubborn ten percent of the mice (whether

Mice and rats show clear paw preference. About half of them are lefties. But most will switch, if necessary, to reach food easily.

they were left-pawed or right-pawed) demonstrated that they would rather fight than switch: they persistently would not, or could not, make use of the opposite paw for easier eating.

Bats (winged cousins of mice and rats) show a preference for the left in one motion: when large groups of them fly out of their caves, they reportedly make use of a left-hand spiral. No one knows why they always fly to the left. This habit certainly prevents mid-air collisions in the crowd—but bats are born with a special "sonar" system that prevents them from bumping into each other (or anything else), anyway.

Elephants, walruses and other mammals with tusks usually have one tusk that is slightly larger (and presumably used more often) than the other. In Africa, elephants are seen digging up roots and tubers with their right tusks more often than the left, and so Africans call the right the "servant tusk."

Apes and monkeys are primates, closely related to human beings. Research on apes such as orangutans, chimpanzees and gorillas has generally shown that these animals are equally proficient with either paw. One individual animal may show a preference for one paw over the other, but this is rare. Most of this population is perfectly ambidexterous. All the results are not in yet, however. Some researchers believe that the higher primates do show some signs of lateralization in brain organization, which is revealed in part by hand use. Monkeys, for ex-

Monkeys and apes (including chimpanzees) seem to be perfectly ambidexterous. Why aren't human beings?

ample, have been observed choosing one paw or the other in a way that is related to the task they are doing: for jobs requiring precision in touch, they tend to use their left paws, but they use their right paws for activities requiring visual coordination. Mountain gorillas in Africa have a skull cavity which (like that of humans) seems to be slightly enlarged on the side of the left hemisphere; these animals favor the right paw for chest-beating.

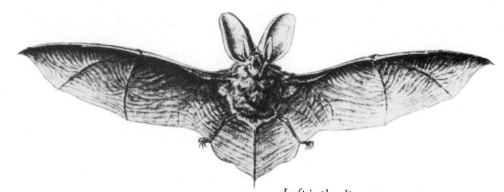

When mammals grow a left and a
right tusk, one is commonly
slightly larger than the other.

Left is the direction preferred by
bats. As they fly out of their cave,
their first turn is always a left-hand
spiral. No one knows why.

Elephants use their tusks for digging up
roots and tubers to eat—and use their
right tusk more often than their left.

What can we conclude from all this? Left-right preferences do exist in the natural world, in inanimate matter, plants and animals, but usually only in structural form. The overwhelming majority of animals exhibit no preference. And if the higher primates are, in the main, ambidexterous, why aren't mice— or human beings? What causes us to make such a clear choice of one hand for preferred use? Credible and incredible theories have been advanced. The answer may one day be found through the study of genetics (heredity), brain organization, intelligence, birth defects, the environment, or our social culture. For the moment, all we can ask is, where does the real answer lie?

Did you know...

...that these famous men are all supposed to have been forcibly-switched sinistrals?

Lewis Carroll

Nelson Rockefeller

Aneurin Bevan

King George VI of Britain

Dr. Samuel Johnson

Are People Born Left-Handed? And Why?

Left-handedness is inherited . . . or that was the assumption, until recently. Left-handedness often runs in families, and therefore it is easy to assume that hand preference is a genetic trait, just like eye color. In the early years of this century, dozens of research projects were conducted and thousands of words were written to support the genetic theory. Then some disquieting facts began to emerge.

In twenty percent of all sets of identical twins, one twin is right-handed and the other is left-handed. Since identical twins are the result of a split embryo, they have *identical genes*, so it seems impossible that their hand preference could be predetermined by heredity. But researchers who believed in the genetic theory persisted in their opinion, and they pointed out that *half* of all children of left-handed parents are also lefties. They agreed that hand preference is controlled by the brain—but they concluded that the right-left pattern of brain dominance is inherited, too.

New research led to new facts. Twice as many males as females are left-handed. And eighty percent of left-handed children are born to two *right*-handed parents. What's the explanation for this?

One startling new theory, developed in the last decade, is that minor brain damage, caused during a stressful birth, makes the baby's brain "switch sides" from right to left. Researchers who support the birth-stress theory offer at least three pieces of evidence. Firsty, baby boys are known to be more vulnerable than girls to stressful births—and, you remember, boys are lefties twice as often as girls. Second, women over thirty years old are likely to have a difficult labor if the baby is their first: and first-born children of mothers over thirty run a higher-than-average chance of being left-handed. Third, twins have a very high percentage of left-handedness. Is it just coincidence that twins are crowded in the womb, may suffer stress there and during birth?

One extra piece of knowledge that seems to fit this theory is the fact that children who have undergone stressful births often have difficulties with language later in life. They stutter or stammer, and they may suffer from dyslexia (impairment of the ability to read). It's well documented that many lefties suffer from exactly these problems, too.

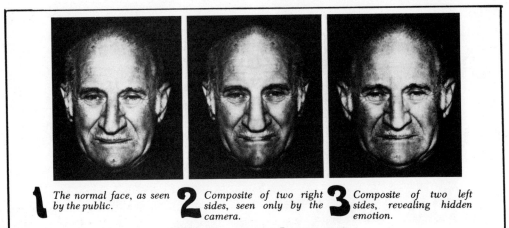

1 *The normal face, as seen by the public.*

2 *Composite of two right sides, seen only by the camera.*

3 *Composite of two left sides, revealing hidden emotion.*

Did you know...

. . . that the left side of your face is supposed to express emotion more intensely than the right? The two sides are not symmetrical (that's been known for years). Photographers can make mirror-image composites of the two right sides of any face, compare the two merged left sides of the same face, and perceive interesting differences. The right side of your face is the side presented to the public. The left side is comparatively private, registering suppressed feelings. Camera tests measuring emotions of unhappiness, surprise, disgust, fear, anger and other feelings all lead to this conclusion.

But—and it's a big BUT, according to researchers who do not agree with the birth-stress hypothesis—is it not probable that the speech problems and reading difficulties suffered by many lefties are caused not by stressful births but by stressful *lives*? The world in which most lefties must live demands constant adaptation to a right-handed (and often hostile) society. It seems clear that these constant demands to adapt could cause frustration and stress in a child. So the third major group of theorists suggests that left-handedness is not inherited and it isn't caused at birth: it is caused by a child's social environment, by psychological conditioning as the child grows up.

Children tend to use both hands interchangeably until they are between three and six years old. Something must happen to make them change, to make most of them stop using their left hands so frequently. If left-handedness is inherited, as the geneticists propose, why is it that only about half of the children born to a duo of left-handed parents turn out to be lefties themselves? Does something happen to make a "natural" lefty switch to using the right hand, instead?

No one can argue that social environment is critical in determining all of a child's preferences. If toys are automatically placed in a baby's right hand, if a baby watches his parents and other children using their right hands, the child learns that the right hand is the hand he or she is *expected* to prefer. Undoubtedly, many children swing to the right because it is easier or more rewarding to fulfill this expectation than to buck it. Think of all the cultural pressures (many of them going back for centuries) that reinforce the use of the right hand. It may be true that southpaws are just that small group of individualists who would rather fight than switch.

Biology is another science in which researchers look for the reason for hand preference. Their field of study is the human brain, particularly the cerebrum, which occupies the topmost portion of the skull and is by far the largest sector of the brain.

In its upper surface (the cerebral cortex), the cerebrum contains most of the master controls of the body. The corpus callosum, a neuron-rich membrane underlying the cerebrum, contains approximately half of the 10 billion (that's 10,000,000,000) nerve cells found in the brain. The cerebral cortex analyzes incoming sensory data as well as all motor impulses that initiate, reinforce, or inhibit the whole spectrum of muscle and gland activity. It's quite a job! What's interesting to us is that the cerebrum, deeply fissured and grooved, is split vertically into left and right hemispheres. The left half of the cerebrum controls the right side of the body; the right half dominates the left side.

One exception to this general rule: whether a person is left- or right-handed, the left hemisphere of the

brain (the "righties' side") in most people—but not all—exerts control over the functions of communication, such as speaking, hearing, and the reading and writing of words.

Scientists observe infants; some of them believe that they can predict, very early in a baby's life, whether the left hemisphere or the right hemisphere of the brain is in control. If the baby tends to lie in a crib in a left-leaning direction, they say, chances are that the right hemisphere is dominant . . . and the child will become a lefty.

A child's obvious choice of hand preference happens at an age when its complex nervous system is growing and maturing. During these years, when a child is learning to control body movements and to reason, there is a growth of myelin—a white, fatty material encasing nerve fibers, also called the "medullary sheath" and sometimes described as the insulation material of the corpus callosum. Does the growth of myelin affect the brain in a way related to the dominant hemisphere? More research has to be done before we know the answer to that one. What we do know is that everything seems to be happening at once to the child between the ages of three and six, who is learning to coordinate muscles, learning to control the bladder, learning to think, and learning that most people prefer to use their right hands.

Man is the only primate to demonstrate a consistent preference for one hand. Human beings, of course, are the only animals that can speak. It seems natural to conclude that there may be some link in our highly developed brains between the two points that control handedness and speech.

As with every complicated question, there may be more than one answer to the question of what makes people lefties. Heredity may very well play a part. Think of the fact that we are not only left- or right-handed, but also have a dominant eye, a dominant leg and foot, even a dominant thumb! Cerebral dominance is obviously related to this apparently automatic preference for one side of the anatomy over the other. Since the 17th century, students of left-handedness have suggested that it is, in some way, connected to the brain. Finally, we cannot ignore the cumulative and powerful effect of more than four thousand years of human history, during which most societies have insisted that right was *right*.

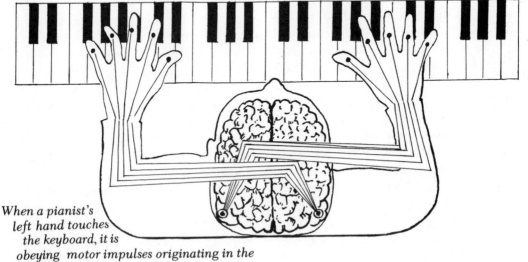

When a pianist's left hand touches the keyboard, it is obeying motor impulses originating in the right side of the cerebral cortex.

More About the Lefty's Brain

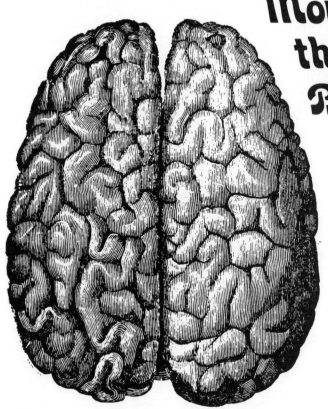

The cerebrum of the brain, a large rounded structure filling most of the cranial cavity, is divided into two hemispheres by a deep central groove. The left hemisphere is usually slightly larger than the right: it controls the right half of the body, and most people, of course, are righties.

When two or more people come to an agreement, they are said to be "of one mind." And although the human brain is split into two halves, its hemispheres are linked by an intricate network of association tracts made up of nerve cells (neurons). So the left and right parts of the brain function as one mind—a marvelous and mysterious unit resembling a complex computer, evaluating and storing millions of pieces of information, controlling and coordinating all our thoughts and actions.

Although the two hemispheres of the cerebrum function as a single unit, each half receives and sends messages from and to different parts of the body. (Our eyes are the only exception to this rule. So that we can see stereoscopically, our left eye and our right eye both send incoming messages to the left *and* the right hemispheres).

Signals to and from the brain usually travel between one hemisphere and the opposite side of the body—between the left hand and the right hemisphere, for example. This fact was discovered and substantiated over a number of years, as doctors and scientists cared for and observed hospital patients and the wounded victims of war. They noticed that damage to the left side of the brain generally resulted in loss of feeling and loss of limb movement on the right side of the body, and vice versa. Further research was done by surgeons who operated on the brain, and by physicians who treated victims of strokes and epileptics. Doctors sometimes cut the corpus callosum of an epileptic patient, in an attempt to sever communication between the two hemispheres of the patient's brain . . . and the amazing result was that the split brain continued to function as a single unit, and the patient could return to his or her normal life.

Brain research over the years has perhaps raised more questions than the answers it has provided. But one fact has become clear: the two hemispheres are not symmetrical, either in the way in which they control the body or even in their size. The left hemisphere is usually slightly larger than the right. For right-handed people, it is the *dominant* hemisphere, but it seems to perform specialized functions even for many lefties. While damage to the left side

Soldiers and hospital patients have been studied for years by doctors, who observe that injury to the brain's left side results in numbness or paralysis of the body's right side. (Union wounded at Fredericksburg, after the battle of May 3, 1863).

of the brain produces serious results —numbness and paralysis on the right side of the body, and perhaps inability to speak—similar damage to the right hemisphere seems to result in inpairments that are less serious and less specific.

One conclusion is that the left hemisphere contains a center controlling our language capabilities— our ability to speak, to read and write. This center normally controls the movements of the right hand for writing. We would expect lefties to follow the same pattern in reverse —to have a language center in their right hemisphere. But no . . . six out of ten lefties have their language center placed *like that of righties*, in the left hemisphere of the cerebrum. A few lefties seem to have control centers for language located in *both* left and right hemispheres; these are the lucky few who could recover unusually quickly from speech impairments caused by a stroke. In many ways, left-handers seem to have a pattern of brain organization that is more diffuse, more dispersed between the two hemispheres, than that of righties. This can sometimes be an advantage; sometimes, it can make life difficult.

Difficulties from which lefties may suffer because of mixed cerebral dominance may include problems with speech, poor muscular coordination, bedwetting, dyslexia (partial "word blindness" or impairment of the ability to read) and other disabilities in learning. Social pressure may also account, to some degree, for these problems.

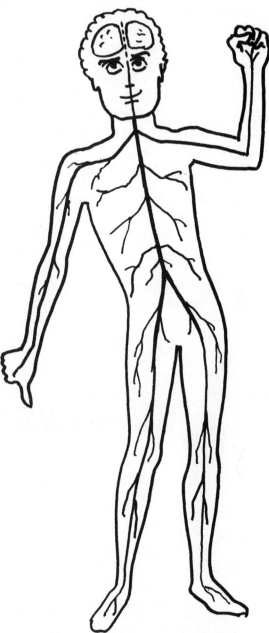

The left hand and the entire left side is controlled by the right hemisphere of the cerebrum. Messages to and from the brain's nerves are sent out to and received from the body's nerves and muscles in a crossed path—from left to right, and from right to left.

65

A left-handed child may be forced to use the right hand for writing and eating, for example, but no parent or teacher can change the fact that important controls in the child's brain will remain where they are natural to a lefty: in the right hemisphere. What happens?—the phenomenon of *cross dominance*, which happens when the naturally-dominant right hemisphere of the brain struggles to transmit and receive signals to and from the "wrong" side of the body, and not in the normal criss-cross direction. Almost all lefties, because of social pressure or because of their diffuse brain organization, suffer to some degree from cross dominance. A total left-hander, with complete dominance located in the right hemisphere, is a rare specimen indeed.

Cross dominance can afflict righties as well as the left-handed. According to statistics, about twenty-five percent of the American population suffers from cross dominance, and a few of these (a minority group within a minority) are right-handed.

"Hooked writing"—writing with the arm crooked away from the body, so that the pen or pencil is held pointing toward the writer and is pulled, rather than pushed, as letters are written—used to be considered a position adopted only by lefties. Theories were that some left-handed children assumed this awkward-looking posture as a result of pressure in schools, as their only solution to teachers' demands that

Did you know...

... that these people trained themselves to be ambidexterous?

Benjamin Franklin

Michelangelo

Sir Daniel Wilson

Sir Edwin Landseer

Leonardo da Vinci

Lord Baden-Powell, British soldier, founder of Boy Scouts.

they shouldn't smear the ink (as their left hand followed the pen, instead of preceding it) and that their lettering should slant in the same direction as that of a right-handed writer. But now researchers have observed that a few right-handers write in this same "hooked" position, mirror-image. The new speculation is that anybody, left-handed or right-handed, who writes like this does not have the usual left-right relationship between hand and brain, but writes in an inverted position because of cross dominance: the language and writing center of control in the brain is probably on the same side as the hand that writes. And that's the fix in which six out

Lefthandedness may be inherited. Queen Victoria (photographed with her son, Edward VII, her grandson, George V, and her great-grandson, Edward VIII) developed her lefthandedness into ambidexterity, as a matter of principle.

A child younger than eight years can switch dominant hemispheres and learn to use the brain's other side, if one half is injured.

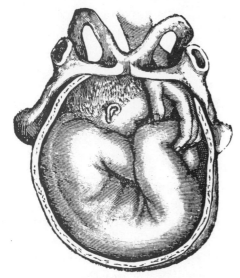

A stressful birth may be one cause of lefthandedness, according to recent scientific theory.

Victoria's great-grandson who inherited her sinistrality as well as her throne was George VI. A switched lefty, King George had a speech defect that made radio broadcasts painfully difficult.

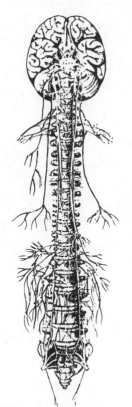

The brain's 10 billion nerves receive messages from the senses and transmit orders to muscles and glands, in a crisscross pattern.

Children tend to use both hands interchangeably, until they are three to six years old. By that age, hand preference is clearly established.

of ten lefties (whether they write "hooked" or not) find themselves.

If the "righties' side" of the brain, the left hemisphere, is the language-control center for most of us, and if it is also the dominant side of the brain for the right-handed majority of the population, then another question comes up. Apart from motor control of muscles and nerves on the left side of the body, what are the functions of the right hemisphere? Is it—as one theory goes—mostly composed of "reserve" grey matter, which will come into use only if the usually dominant left hemisphere is injured?

When accident or disease damages a child's brain in its dominant hemisphere, the child—especially if it is younger than eight years old—can generally switch sides and relearn speech and other functions by using the other hemisphere. This "take-over" ability gave credence to the theory that one side of the brain performs most necessary functions, and that the second hemisphere is largely unused. The "takeover" seems easier, moreover, if the damaged hemisphere is the left—the language center, and the dominant side for most righties.

If the "lefties side," the right hemisphere, is injured, no one knows, yet, whether or not the left hemisphere can fully compensate for the damage. More research needs to be done. In the meantime, scientists and researchers in many fields continue to ask: what are the real functions of the right hemisphere of the cerebrum?

The right hemisphere, according

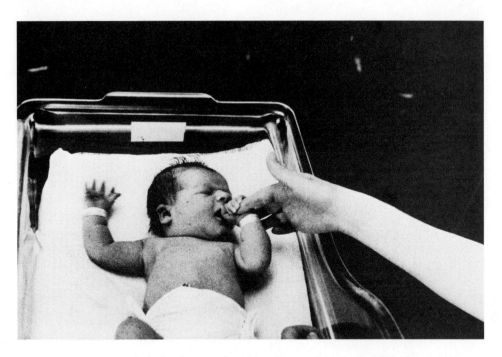

*A baby's ultimate hand preference can be predicted
very early in life, some scientists believe.*

to a theory developed around 1962 by Dr. Roger Sperry of the California Institute of Technology, specializes in the analysis of perceptions of space, of musical tones, of aesthetic judgment, and in the ability to integrate component parts or fractions of something into a complete systematic entity, regardless of the lapses of time. Lefties can excel when creativity, insight and intuition are what's needed. The functions of the left half of the brain, in contrast, seem more verbal and analytical, mathematical and logical, related to thought processes that are linear and sequential.

Lefties may be free to be the dreamers and creators in our society. Three hundred and fifty years ago, an English physican and inventor named Robert Fludd postulated that the human mind was a universe in miniature—a brain with sections for intellect (corresponding to God), for imagination (Man) and for sensation (Earth). Recently, neurosurgeon Joseph Bogen has summarized current theories about the brain with another graceful metaphor: the left hemisphere sees the person existing in the world, while the right hemisphere (the lefty's half) sees the world existing in the person.

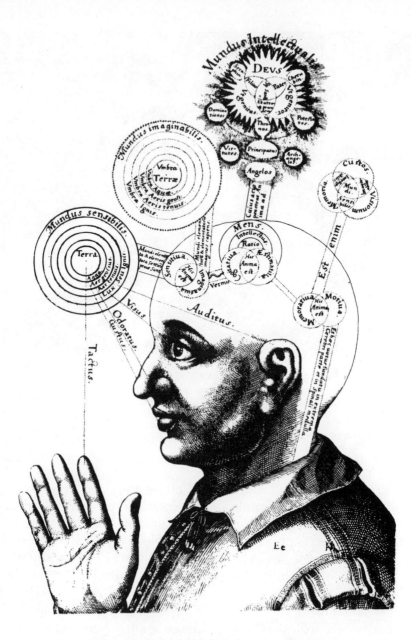

350 years ago, an English doctor saw the human mind as a miniature universe. Recent theories differentiate between the dominant hemispheres of the lefty's and the righty's brain.

Are You Sure You're a Lefty?

[OR RIGHT-HANDED?]

Many people who think of themselves as lefties are not totally left-handed. Others who have been convinced since childhood that they are right-handed, may, in fact, be "switched lefties" and never know it.

To be a switched lefty without knowing it can amount to an affliction. The story of one such person—writer Andreas de Rhoda, who discovered his secret only with his wife's help—was published in *The Christian Science Monitor*, and is reprinted here with permission.

"As long as I can think back, I have shuddered at the thought of doing manual work. My parents did their best to introduce me to its pleasures; Father, in his hobby workshop, tried to show me how to build and carve tea tables, dust-cloth holders and bird feeders; Mother, in her *Gemusegarten*, tried to charm me into growing cucumbers and communing with nature."

"All in vain. The phobia i entertained about using my hands for anything other than turning book pages, paddling canoes, and eating was patently incurable and everyone knew why: I was unspeakably clumsy and didn't care to be reminded of it."

"During an air raid on Bremen in 1943, I did manage to restore the electric light in our basement bomb shelter by tightening a loose screw in a plug. Mother sent up a prayer of thanks for a modern-day miracle. Father speculated that the shock of the raid had somehow unsnapped my mental bonds. Both were proved wrong when, minutes later at the end of the raid, I almost broke off the doorhandle on my way out by turning it the wrong way."

"I might have never learned the cause of my affliction if it hadn't been for Catarina. She placed her finger squarely on it after the first three weeks of our marriage ten years ago.

" 'You, darling,' she announced, 'are left-handed.' "

" 'And you, darling, have just cracked the poorest-kept secret of my family. If there had been a Knight's Cross with Diamond Clusters for Clumsiness, I would have been the first to be decorated therewith.' "

" 'I mean it literally,' she insisted. 'You are left-handed and you don't even know it. You have been suppressing that since you were weaned.' "

"Coldly, with the rational compassion of someone who knows she must hurt to heal, she marshalled the evidence; several times a day she said she had to replace the telephone which I had left in its cradle in the way only left-handed people do; she had been untying wires around plastic bags twisted invariably to the left instead of to the right. And so on and so forth. She followed the trail of my latent, blatant sinistrality from the kitchen into the living room into the bathroom into the study into the bedroom and out into the bicycle room, with the expertise of a she-Lieutenant Columbo."

" 'So, naturally,' she summed up, 'you are not clumsy. You are frustrated, suppressed. In short, unliberated.'

"I stared at her unbelieving. I didn't recall a single instance of having been kept from using my left hand as a child. If I was, it must have been too early to recall. But back in Germany in those days there wasn't quite as much tolerance to left-handedness—or to anything else for that matter—as there has been in the United States. Since I've come here I've seen hundreds of people write with their left; I watched President Ford do it in the Rose Garden on TV. And I feel again the inexplicable pain that comes with observing him or anyone else do it. Suppressed? Might she be right?"

" 'Just watch your hands,' she advised. 'You'll see.' "

"I did and I saw. The first thing I saw was that nearly all the bloopers that come up on my typewriter involve letters controlled not by my left but by my right."

"In the decade since, I have seen my left hand act in strangely self-assertive ways without any prompting or even desire on my part: quietly striking out in spontaneous initiatives; taking a pot to fill a cup held by the right; turning light switches on and off as if I had done it all my life; doing a host of chores that had once been the strict prerogative of the right."

"Yesterday, while digging up the front lawn, I tossed the shaken-out grass sods and the larger stones into a bucket some ten feet away, a feat of precision I had never achieved, before I realized I was

The typewriter is one of the few truly unbiased machines. In fact, many of the most frequently used keys are at your left.

doing it with my left. (As a boy I had to go home when others started playing ball; I couldn't catch more than one out of ten nor aim them. It was attributed to faulty vision.)"

"Vision, my eye. That moment in the garden yesterday, an unknown sense of freedom and of peace bubbled up in me, a seltzer of joy from a hidden spring. Something alien has been befriended; something lost has been found; something guilty has been redeemed. And miracle upon miracles: I have come to enjoy growing cucumbers in Catarina's *Gemusegarten!*"

Tests

In case you suspect that you may be suffering from the same affliction as Andreas de Rhoda—unacknowledged left-handedness—we have compiled some quick, easy tests to help you determine which side of your body (eye, foot and leg, as well as hand) is naturally dominant.

#1: HANDS:

Quickly clasp your hands together, interlocking fingers. Do it without looking. Now look down at your hands. Which thumb is on top of the other?

#2: HANDS:

Get a pencil and a sheet of paper. Now draw two circles—one with your right hand, one with your left. Now look at the *direction* in which you drew the circles: clockwise? counterclockwise? one of each?

#3: HANDS:

With pencil and paper still in hand, think of a friend of yours. Now quickly and simply sketch his or her face, in *profile*. Don't worry about realistic details ... artistic skill doesn't matter. But note: which hand are you drawing with?

#4: EYES:

Punch a small hole (but not so small that you can't see through it) in an 8″ × 10″ sheet of typing paper. Locate a small object (a door handle, a light switch) about twelve feet away from you. Hold the paper, with both your hands, at arm's length. Looking through the hole, keep your eyes on the object while you slowly move the paper toward your face, then move it away to arm's length, again. Repeat this movement several times. Does the hole in the paper always end up in front of one eye? Which?

#5: EYES:

Roll up your sheet of paper to make a small funnel-shaped device like a megaphone or bullhorn. Without

We have a dominant leg and foot, even a dominant eye—all often matched to our hand and arm preference. Try these test to locate your dominant foot.

thinking—quickly—bring it toward you and peek at some object, looking through the *large* end. Which eye did you use?

#6: FEET:

Crumple up the piece of paper into a ball. Throw it on the floor, in the middle of the room, away from furniture. Now run toward it and kick it. Which foot did you use?

#7: FEET:

Stand in the middle of the room. Slowly lean forward, so far that you start to fall, off balance. Stop yourself from falling, naturally, by putting one foot out in front of your body to brace yourself. Which foot did you move?

#8: FEET:

Look at your shoes. Most people tend to bear down harder on the left side or the right side of the sole and heel.

#9: FEET:

Measure your feet for length, and for breadth. Are they both exactly the same size . . . or is one very slightly larger than the other?

#10: ARMS:

Take the same ruler or tape measure. Measure both your arms. Are they exactly the same length?

#11: LEGS:

Sit down. Quickly, without thinking about it, cross your legs. Done? Now look down. Which leg is uppermost?

The last tests won't *prove* anything . . . but they may give righties a little more compassion for the plight of southpaw writers. And they may demonstrate how lefties have been taught to become adaptable.

#12: JUST FOR FUN:

On an 8″ × 10″ sheet of plain paper, draw a five-pointed star with a single line, like this:

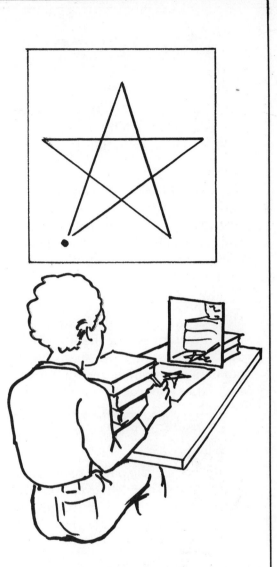

Now place the sheet of paper below a mirror, on a desk or table top. Face the mirror, but make a screen (of a tilted large envelope, or a pile of books, for example) so that you cannot see the original piece of paper—only its image in the mirror. Like this:—

Now pick up your pencil, and try to follow the lines you made when you originally drew the star so easily.

#13: JUST FOR FUN:

Press a sheet of paper against your forehead. Now write your own name, from left to right.

#14: JUST FOR FUN:

Try mirror writing. Write a sentence in reverse image, so that you think it can be read in a mirror. Try this with both hands. Which is easier? What is the meaning of your responses to the tests?

The answers to these tests are all on the next page. But don't cheat! Try the tests before you turn the page; otherwise, you may influence your own response, and you'll never know whether or not you're really a lefty. Make a note of your responses, and *then* turn the page.

Answers

#1: HANDS:

Is the hand with the uppermost thumb your left hand? If so, chances are that you are a lefty—even if you write with your right hand.

#2: HANDS:

If with either hand you drew a *clockwise* circle, you have some tendencies toward left-handedness. Most people who are completely right-handed will draw both circles counterclockwise.

#3: HANDS:

If your drawn profile faces in the same direction as the hand which you drew it, you have some cross dominance in your brain functions. Most lefties will sketch a profile facing right, and right-handers will draw a profile facing left.

#4: EYES:

If the hole in the paper repeatedly comes up to your left eye, you are probably left-eyed. If it comes to your right eye, of course your right eye is dominant.

#5: EYES:

You know the answer. The eye you chose is the dominant one.

#6: FEET:

Your foot preference will usually match your hand preference.

#7: FEET:

The foot you instinctively move forward, to prevent yourself from falling, is assumed to be on your stronger, dominant, side.

#8: FEET:

Check not only the shoes that you are wearing, but also those in your closet. See if a pattern of wearing is consistent. The side that is consistently worn down, on all your shoes, is the clue to the dominant side of your body.

#9: FEET:

Chances are that the larger foot is the dominant one, and a clue to the dominant side of your whole body.

10: ARMS:

If you are left-handed, your left arm will probably be a few fractions of an inch longer than your right.

#11: LEGS:

If the upper leg is uppermost, there is a great probability that you are left-legged, left-sided, and left-handed. If you are left-eyed, you are a member of that small breed: a total *lefty*.

#12: JUST FOR FUN:

This should be a lesson in the complex coordination between brain, eye and hand.

#13: JUST FOR FUN:

Whichever hand you wrote with, the signature probably came out in the "wrong" direction, like mirror-image writing.

#14: JUST FOR FUN:

If you are a real lefty, this will probably have been easier for you than if you are right-handed. If you can do mirror-writing quickly, effortlessly and correctly, chances are that you—like Leonardo da Vinci—are very strongly left-oriented.

Casey Stengel was
as well known for the
famous wink that closed
his non-dominant eye
as for his southpaw.

Lefties find it natural
to draw a profile
facing right. This
portrait of Baudelaire
by Edouard Manet
raises a question: was
Manet a lefty, or
was he just observing
his friend in this
position?

Is one of your feet slightly longer
and wider than the other?
Chances are that it's on the
dominant side of your body.

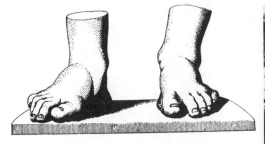

The foot you instinctively
use to kick a ball or to stop
yourself from falling will
usually be on the same side as
your dominant hand.
(Lefty soccer star Pelé).

The Lefty's Personal

W. C. FIELDS • ALBERT EINSTEIN • NELSON ROCKEFELLER • KATE JACKSON

and Professional Life

BILLY THE KID • MICHELANGELO • JOHN DILLINGER • QUEEN VICTORIA

For a lefty to live with a righthanded mate isn't easy. Their basic thought processes are different. Calm explanations during conflict may show that both people were really making the same point.

Living with a Lefty

Many righties find themselves loving and living with a member of the left-handed minority. And it's not uncommon for right-handed parents to produce a left-handed child. If you aren't a southpaw yourself, the next best thing, in our opinion, is loving one. But there are times when you may find that having a lefty on the premises is a bit baffling, or challenging, depending on how you look at life.

Remember that lefties are *different:* they are supposed to be unusually intuitive and creative (instead of rational and analytical), to see the "big picture" (instead of analyzing its parts), to assess the world in terms of space and proportions (not in terms of time), and to be less verbal than righties. If you are an astute righty, remembering these generalities may make your life with a lefty a little easier.

But don't forget that individual lefties may be as different from one another as W. C. Fields and Albert Einstein . . . or Queen Victoria and John Dillinger.

The right hemisphere of the brain remains, to some extent, a mystery to scientific researchers. So it's not surprising that a lefty's thought processes may sometimes baffle an average right-hander. But remember, righties, lefties may feel that way about *your* way of thinking. Often, a few calm explanations are necessary before a lefty and a righty understand that they are both making the same point.

Lefties can take pride in the fact that experts agree they are staunch individualists—independent, self-reliant and often skeptical. They are unwilling to conform, because they are less likely than righties to believe what they are told: this is one con-

. . . that cranks of all kinds are among the implements and tools that southpaws find persistently difficult to use?

clusion from studies conducted at Boston University. Because of these characteristics, lefties have made significant contributions and decisions that have changed the world. Just one example of the type of the skeptical southpaw is the former U.S. President, Harry S. Truman—an independent thinker from a town called Independence, in Missouri (the state known as the "Show Me" State).

But these nonconformist qualities have also led to the fact that lefties have sometimes been labeled "socially maladjusted." Skepticism and a fierce sense of independence

A prototype of the independent-minded, skeptical and stubborn lefty was President Harry S. Truman. (Queen Elizabeth, daughter of two lefties, is righthanded—but has a lefthanded heir).

may well make a lefty argumentative, especially if he or she is being given orders. And a lefty may be moody, easily depressed or apt to drink too much alcohol: that can be blamed on the particular sensitivities of the dominant right hemisphere of the brain.

Give your lefty plenty of emotional space. Research has shown that southpaws resist situations and people who attempt to restrict their lifestyle or to crowd and pressure them in some manner. And keep in mind that a lefty who won't easily follow the mob—or you—may take a little adjusting to, but will certainly add spice to your life. Lefties and righties living together have an opportunity denied people of the same handedness. They *have* to learn tolerance and they can benefit from daily seeing the "other side." Lefties tend to be adaptable (society forces them to be at least partially ambidexterous), and they may show the righties who live with them their own potential for adaptability.

Even if you are a right-handed saint, you will inevitably have conflicts with the lefty in your life— whether he or she is friend or spouse, parent or child. As Dr. Lawson G. Lowrey, former editor of *The American Journal of Orthopsychiatry*, has summed it up: "Left-handed people have been described as temperamental, unstable, unintelligent, pugnacious. . . ." These personality traits occur in right-handed people too, he points out. And it's wise to bear in mind that the supposedly typical and troublesome

Lefties are typically pugnacious and stubborn . . . or, depending on how you see them, feisty and independent. (Casey Stengel arguing with an umpire, 1960).

characteristics of your lefty can be seen—in other situations—as sound virtues. A lefty whom you're tempted to call "pugnacious" could be considered plain "feisty," and "creative" or "innovative" instead of "temperamental." The meaning of the words you use to describe your lefty (even to yourself) may make a great deal of difference to the friendship or love you share.

Instead of calling your lefty:
>
> *stubborn*
> *rebellious*
> *different*
> *slow*
> *plodding*
> *skeptical* or
> *socially maladjusted,*

consider that he or she may be:
>
> *independent*
> *willing to go it alone*
> *original*
> *thoughtful*
> *persistent*
> *questioning* and
> *nonconformist.*

If the lefty in your life is your lover, you can make life a little sweeter by carefully observing whether or not he or she is totally left-sided (left-eyed, left-legged, as well as left-handed). If your mate does prove to be a total lefty, auditory stimulation will be greater in the left ear . . . so that's the ear in which to whisper your sweet nothings for maximum effect.

In your home, make as much space as you can for the creative interests of the typical lefty—painting and sculpture, music and dancing, or athletic exercise. And provide as many simple conveniences as possible. Arrange furniture and major appliances so that they can most easily be used by both the left-handed and the right-handed in the household. If you are buying a new refrigerator, for example, consider the merits of a left-opening or a right-opening door from the viewpoint of the lefty as well as your own. Organize closets to minimize awkwardness for the lefty who has to move clothes or utensils on and off hangers or in and out of drawers and shelf space.

If your love is a lefty, whisper sweet nothings into the left ear. That's where auditory stimulation is greater. (Illustration from **Peter Pan** *by lefty Sir James Barrie).*

Standing lamps and desk lamps are effective only when they are correctly placed. When a lefty is reading, writing, sewing or doing other tasks that require good light,

The problem: when righties and a lefty share the same side of a dining table, meal times become a conflict of jostling elbows.

The solution: seat left-handed guests or family members at the end of the table, to give them elbow room.

the lamp must be positioned so that the light shines over his or her *right* shoulder.

Seating arrangements at the dining table are a very important (and often overlooked) consideration. When a lefty and a right share the same side of the table, meal times can become a conflict of jostling elbows. The more crowded the table, the more exaggerated the problem becomes. When left-handed guests are invited, a sensitive host or hostess will try to seat them at the *end* of a side of a rectangular table: that way, the left elbow is free to move outward without jabbing a neighboring right-handed eater in the ribs. The next-best position for a lefty is on the right-hand of the right-handed eater at the end of the row: if elbow jostling occurs there, the righty on the outside is free to wriggle a little further away and to create more space between them. Of course, the easiest solution is to invite only left-handers for dinner, but that isn't often possible. As one of our southpaw friends expressed the problem: "There are so many of THEM!"

When traveling with a lefty, let him or her sit in the aisle seat when you're on the right side of an airplane, bus, or train ... or in the window seat, when you're on the left side. That way, you will both eat in comfort.

At home, equip your household with as many as possible of the utensils and tools specially designed for southpaws (see the catalog section at the end of this book). Some of these make appreciated presents. Other purchases may be a simple matter of physical safety: many pieces of equipment designed for righties are dangerous as well as difficult for lefties to use. Think of this as you buy tools for the home, garden and workshop.

Many accidents happen in the bathroom and bedroom, but for the southpaw the kitchen is often the most treacherous room of all. Preparing a meal or doing other domestic chores with right-handed equipment can mean cuts, spills and burns for a lefty. Electrical appliances (portable mixers and irons, for example) nearly always have the electric cord emerging on the side that is out of the way for a right-handed user. For a lefty, the cord passes between the appliance and the person using it— a potentially hazardous arrangement. Some appliances have cord attachments which may simply be changed from one side to the other with a screw driver. This is especially useful on an iron. If you can't find these interchangeable connections on an appliance, look for a brand which has the cord attached to the center rear.

Cuts happen easily when a lefty peels vegetables or fruits with a right-handed parer. Whipping cream or eggs with an opposite-turning beater can literally mean egg on

For a lefty, the kitchen may be the most dangerous room in the house. Frying pans and ladles with pouring lips only on the righty's side force a lefthanded cook to pour backhanded.

your face. It's hard for a lefty to keep a firm grip on a can while struggling to open it with a right-handed can-opener—and that may mean a dropped can and a bruised foot. Deceptive mitten-shaped oven gloves may be insulated only for the palm side as worn by a right-handed cook. Slip the same glove on to the left hand, and you can get a very hot, painful surprise. Frying pans and ladles with a pouring lip only on the righty's side demand that a left-handed cook pour backhanded and risk spilling hot liquid.

Private disasters in the kitchen can be followed by embarrassingly public fumbles in the dining room. A corkscrew, for example, turns clockwise: a lefty trying to open a bottle of wine may try to turn it counterclockwise, be jabbed by the sharp point as the opener slips, and perhaps even break the bottle. The supreme insult is that—after all these painful mishaps—guests and family will conclude that you are *clumsy!*

In the workshop, power saws are particularly dangerous—for any user. But a lefty obscures his or her line of sight, as the saw is being used. Wood turning lathes present similar problems. Power drills often have trigger locks on the left side. They may inadvertently be turned on when the tool is held in the left hand. Even out in the garden, pruning shears and other instruments with sharp edges and controls on the "wrong" side may be dangerous. Watch out.

Did you know...

. . . these famous lefties?

Isaac Hayes
Jimi Hendrix
Rod Steiger
Casey Stengel
Terry Thomas

Steve McQueen
Martha Mitchell

Sandy Koufax

Gentler crafts and hobbies, quietly pursued at a desk or in an armchair in the living room, would be safer and easier for the lefty in your household, perhaps. Not so. Some of them—with instructions all geared for the right-handed—are frustrating enough to result in short tempers and ulcers.

Unless the lefty is lucky enough to have had a left-handed grandparent or camp counselor to show him or her how to knit, crochet, do needlework and calligraphy and woodwork left-handed, the effort to learn from printed instructions (or from a right-handed instructor) may be frustrating, difficult, even impossible.

Luckily, in the last five years or so this problem has come to light. If you want to learn to knit—and you're able to read instructions in French or some other language of continental Europe (not the British Isles)—adopt the method called Continental knitting, in which the left hand manipulates the working needle. For help with knitting and other crafts, contact the lefty stores and mail-order catalogs listed in the last chapter of this book, and look in our bibliography for details about special publications. Look at the back of our book, too, for special equipment—such as the Sears' mini drill press which is designed to be adjustable for either left-handed or right-handed crafts people working with wood or metal.

There are surprisingly few books to help you if the lefty in your household is your child. With all the books on "parenting" currently published, it is astonishing that so little information or advice has so far been provided for the parents of a young southpaw. In our bibliography at the end of this book, you will find listed a few books on teaching left-handed children how to overcome difficulties with writing, reading, dyslexia and stuttering. One academic publication intended primarily for psychologists is *The Sinister Child* by Blau. A book written (nearly twenty years ago) to help a child understand what it's like to be left-handed is *Lefty*, by Dr. Marguerite Rush Lerner; another is *The Left-hander's World* by Dr.

Did you know

. . . that seeing a new moon over your left shoulder will bring you good luck?

Alvin Silverstein and Virginia B. Silverstein (for ages 9 and older).

We have all heard stories about famous people whose parents forced them to change from natural left-handedness to using the right hand, thereby causing lifelong problems. Lewis Carroll stammered. So did King George VI. The former Vice President of the United States, Nelson Rockefeller, had difficulty reading a prepared speech. "Few people were aware of the problem, but all his life he suffered from an innate tendency to read backward from right to left, a difficulty that may have had its origin in his father's unrelenting effort to change young Nelson from a left-hander to a right-hander," reported the writer of his obituary in *The New York Times*. "Around the family dinner table," the reporter related, "the elder Mr.

Nelson Rockefeller was a switched lefty. It is thought this contributed to his dyslexia, an affliction which made reading a speech a life-long problem.

Rockefeller would put a rubber band around his son's left wrist, tie a long string on it and jerk the string whenever Nelson started to eat with his left hand, the one he naturally favored." The result? "Eventually, the boy achieved a rather awkward ambidextrous compromise."

Well, that unhappy childhood was nearly seventy years ago. Today, the key phrase for parents of a pre-school lefty is *benign neglect.* Observe and help your child, if he or she needs help. Do not make an issue over hand preference. As far as possible, encourage the use of both hands, in order to prepare your child for coping with a predominantly right-handed world. If your child is clearly a lefty, you can help by

buying a few pieces of special equipment, such as left-handed scissors.

How can you be sure that your child really is a lefty? The first clue is in the family tree: if parents or grandparents are left-handed, chances are high that the baby will be a lefty, too. If the child is one of twins, chances are even higher.

During the first few months of a baby's life, you may see some clues to the hand preference which will show itself more clearly in later years. Watch to see which side the infant leans toward in the crib, on to which side the baby most naturally rolls, which hand tends to grasp for objects. During the first two or three years of childhood, which hand normally performs an active task?

Which foot does the child use to kick a ball with? Which eye seems to be predominant? Foot and eye dominance are often linked to hand preference.

Some experts contend that if the child is under six years old, if the child uses both hands with equal skill, and if the child is above average in intelligence, then use of the right hand should be encouraged during a trial period. If difficulties result, the parents should stop this experiment instantly.

Other experts (and we agree with them) say that hand preference should simply be allowed to develop naturally. Once a young child has shown a clear choice of one hand for eating, scribbling, waving and throwing a ball, then use of the chosen hand should be encouraged as skills develop.

Being aware of the possibility of left-handedness will make you sensitive to possible problems. Watch your child's control of small muscles. Does he or she find it difficult to hold a cup or a crayon? Lack of small-muscle control is linked to development of the brain's cortex and may be connected to left-handedness. If your child seems to have difficulty with coordination, it may be a neurological problem related to hand, foot and eye preference. Watch, but do not overreact. Many people, both left- and right-handed, suffer from cross dominance in brain patterns. If your child seems to have problems with coordination, it may be that you have a left-handed child using his or her

Which side of a crib will a baby turn toward? Watch carefully. The chosen direction may indicate the naturally dominant side of the child's body.

Clues to hand preference, and to a dominant foot and eye as well, may be seen in the first months of a baby's life.

If a young child consistently prefers the left hand for eating, scribbling or waving, use of that hand should be encouraged as skills develop.

right eye, or vice versa. The relationship between hand preference and eye preference can easily be tested by a doctor. If there is a significant discrepancy here, your child can be trained by an eye doctor or at a reading clinic to use the eye on the same side as the dominant hand.

How does your child walk? Most people walk with a rhythmical cross pattern, swinging the left arm forward with the right leg, the right arm forward with the left leg. Homolateral walking—moving forward the arm that's on the same side as the leg—is a sign of neurological disorganization. If this pattern persists, check with a neurologist.

Most children no longer have problems with bed wetting after they are three years old. But left-handed children suffer from particular difficulties in controlling their bladders. No one really knows why; not enough research has been done. Some scientists attribute the problem to cross-dominant messages from the brain, which sends two signals to the bladder: *open* or *close*. If the child is right-handed, the bladder receives and complies with these messages from the dominant left hemisphere of the brain. But a lefty may have a pattern of mixed dominance, and the bladder may receive messages from both sides of the brain. The result is confusion. Accidents occur. There is no solution except patience and understanding, and confidence on the parent's part that the problem will in almost all cases resolve itself as the child learns control.

. . . that there is an International Lefthanders Day? Promoted by Lefthanders International, the annual celebration is August 13th.

Left-handedness is usually more of a simple inconvenience than the cause of any significant problem. Don't try to force your left-handed child to adopt right-handed skills—you'll succeed only in creating emotional disturbances, such as difficulties with speech and reading. Your job as a parent is to make your child's life easier in the small details of daily life, such as buttoning clothes, tying shoe laces, cutting with scissors. You may try to teach your child by asking him or her to mimic the motions of your own hands. If you're a righty and your child's a lefty, remember that this won't work easily. Try mirror teaching, which is as much fun as a game. Face the child, tell him or her to imagine that you are a reflection in a mirror and then to imitate what you do.

Above all, don't fret if your child has trouble, at first, with simple tasks. Learning takes time.

Arithmetic poses fewer problems than reading and writing for the lefty in school.

The Lefty at School

Many children three and four years old attend kindergarten or nursery school, where they learn to use crayons, scissors, paints and construction paper. These activities may encourage development of hand preference. "The first real problem a left-handed child has to face is the difficulty of using scissors," reports the catalog of Anything Left Handed, of London. "The natural effect of using right-handed scissors is that the left hand tends to force the blades apart so that no cutting takes place. The smaller the hand, the more pronounced is this action." Some children develop hand preference—and face their first struggles with tools like scissors—later than others. But by the age of five or six, when most children start school, hand choice has generally been established. You will know, by then, whether your child will be a southpaw for life.

And this is when your real work as the parent of a lefty begins. It might be wise to read together a story about left-handedness (such as Lerner's *Lefty*), to reassure your child that being different because of being a lefty is not a handicap . . . it's natural, special, in some cases even an advantage.

There's no need to worry about arithmetic in the first year of school. But the other two of the three Rs—reading and 'riting—may present a few problems. The problems may be caused by the teacher (although there *are* left-handed teachers, of course, as well as right-handed teachers sympathetic to lefty pupils). More likely, problems may be caused by the school system which, like the Army, insists on some measure of conformity. This means that, although lefties aren't forced to change their handedness any more, their particular needs will not be catered to. Although left-handed children should not be treated in a way that singles them out as being unusual, according to psychologist Theodore H. Blau, an ideal educational environment would encourage their needs for freedom and individuality. They shouldn't be forced to conform to a right-handed system.

Did you know...

...these famous lefties?

Anthony Newley
Arnold Palmer

Joanne Woodward
Keenan Wynn

Thothmes III

Euell Gibbons
Paul Michael Glaser

Richard Dreyfuss

Reading is a difficult skill for many a child—lefty or righty—to learn. Over-anxious parents sometimes demand more than is realistic of a child at a given age. Parents of a lefty are particularly prone to anxious doubts when—after years of boasting that their child is unusually "creative," "precocious," "smart for his age" and so forth—the offspring suddenly hits a barrier and has difficulty in learning to read and to write.

The ability to learn these skills correlates with a child's growth—physical growth, emotional growth and growth in social behavior. The senses of sight and hearing must be properly developed, of course. Equally important: the nervous system must be developed to the point where movements can be controlled, and the language center must be developed in one or other of the brain's hemispheres. The child needs to have established a dominant hand, and preferably a dominant eye.

The boastful clucking of parents of so-called "advanced" offspring tends to obscure the fact that physical and mental growth varies from child to child, and that the speed of learning has little bearing on the child's real intelligence and potential mental capabilities.

Lefties learn to *speak* language as quickly and easily as right-handed children. But when it comes to reading and writing it—especially if it's a language, like English, written from left to right across the page—the left often has problems. Here comes the word feared by many parents: dyslexia.

Dyslexia means, quite simply, "difficulty in learning to read and write." (The real but rare inability to read, "word blindness," is called alexia). Dyslexia is an impairment that afflicts about 28% of the general population, and the overwhelming majority of the sufferers are right-handed. But it's true that lefties are twice as likely as righties to suffer from dyslexia. Why? Probably just because our language is written and read from left to right, and a lefty's natural tendency is to scan a page from right to left.

A lefty will tend to look at the last letter of a word first, and to see the first letter last. For example: the letters of the word BOOK may be observed, in order, as KOOB. In addition to this problem of an unnatural left-to-right direction, a lefty is confronted with an alphabet filled with letters that look like mirror images of each other, and which can easily cause confusion: b/d; p/q; w/m. If your natural inclination is to read from right to left, you may see "was" as "saw," or "on" as "no," and so forth. When a lefty child tries to spell a word, the letters may come out backwards, and even the order of words in a sentence may be reversed or confused.

What can be done? The left-to-right pattern conventional in our culture has to be superimposed over the child's natural inclination for right-to-left. Parents may buy publications on remedial reading and writing, several of which are listed in our bibliography at the end of this book. Teachers must be encouraged to use methods of study to encourage the dyslexic child: tracing from left to right; using writing paper with brightly colored left margins; making frequent reference to the direction of the movement in our letters, words and sentences. The teachers (and parents) need patience, the freedom to "*over*-teach," and the real understanding that dyslexia is

Dyslexic children can be helped to read and write by being taught to swim—an activity which coordinates brain and muscles on the left and right.

Many children reverse the shape of the letters "s" and "n" as they learn to write. Lefties, who may perceive letters and even whole words in mirror image, can easily confuse "b" and "d", "p" and "q", "w" and "m".

a film starring Charlie Chaplin, Rock Hudson or Cary Grant, and having that shock of awareness when the actor began to write—with his left hand. If you are a lefty yourself, you tend to be specially aware of another person's writing hand.

Unlike throwing a ball, which can be regarded as an innate action, writing is a skill that has been taught to you. If you write left-handed, your instinct to be a lefty is stronger than social pressures on you to change to right-handedness. You have successfully resisted equipment and teaching methods that have, for centuries, been designed exclusively for righties. Only very recently has this started to change.

In the past, left-handed writers were reprimanded for being sloppy or clumsy. But sloppiness was the fault of the equipment: before the

simply a problem of delivering information to a brain naturally patterned to resist it—not, in any way, an affliction that reflects badly on the child's real capability and intelligence. Parents should try to ensure that their schools have provisions for the special teaching of dyslexics. Above all, they themselves should stay calm, and prevent the problem from becoming a stressful situation for the child. Make books as much fun as possible, at home as well as in school.

Writing poses problems for lefties, too. In the first place, it's in the instant when you reach for a pen or pencil, and begin to write or draw with your left hand, that other people become aware of your difference: that you are a lefty. We've all had the experience of watching

In classrooms, chairs with desk-arms to the left as well as to the standard right must be provided.

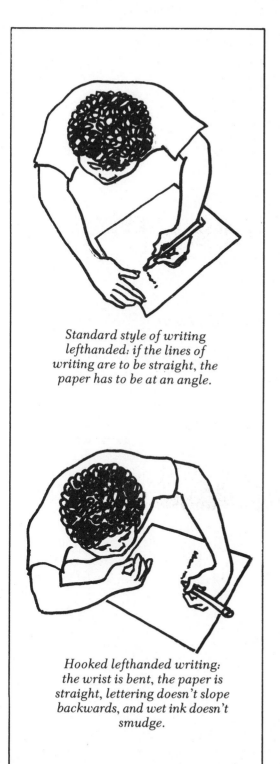

Standard style of writing lefthanded: if the lines of writing are to be straight, the paper has to be at an angle.

Hooked lefthanded writing: the wrist is bent, the paper is straight, lettering doesn't slope backwards, and wet ink doesn't smudge.

days of ballpoint pens and quick-drying ink, writing was a difficult task for southpaws. Right-handers "pull" the pen or pencil across the page, while lefties have to "push" it. The nibs of fountain pens used to be designed exclusively for righties and they would snag on the surface of the paper when pushed by the left hand. Small blots and splatters happened. The left hand would also smudge the wet ink as it passed across words that had just been written.

Modern writing materials have provided solutions for inadvertent sloppiness. But other problems remain—problems caused when lefties are not given special instruction in how to write, but are merely told to imitate the motions of righties. Lefties may resolve one difficulty—preventing their lettering from slanting "backwards," or to the left—by writing with arm and hand curved in hooked position. Recent research has shown that a substantial number of righties, as well as about half of all southpaws, naturally write best in a hooked posture and that this may be related to patterns of brain organization.) Another explanation for hooked writing is that it enables lefties to position their paper straight, as righties do. Teachers, left-handed or right-handed, should be shown how to *help* their lefty students write correctly and easily.

Without proper help, a lefty may write with a cramped style and at very slow speed. And this spells TROUBLE. Students with poor handwriting may be discriminated against

Schools in all nations used to compel children to write righthanded. The result for a lefty was a blotted copybook and, often, emotional problems.

in the grading of tests or essays where "penmanship" is a factor. If speed in taking notes or writing exams is important, there's another disadvantage for lefties. F. Lee Bailey, the famous trial lawyer, was a brilliant student, but he scored poorly in his classes in criminal law—simply because he couldn't write his exams quickly enough. Bailey's problem was resolved when he was allowed to use a typewriter.

Not all left-handed students are so lucky. Many school systems resist special dispensations from standard equipment and rules. It's important that parents of young lefties do whatever they can to make sure that their youngsters acquire good writing skills—that they learn to write as easily, quickly and legibly as righties.

Key points for a student learning to write with the left hand:

(1) The writing surface should be comfortable. There should be plenty of space to the student's left. In classrooms, chairs with desk-arms to the *left* as well as to the standard right should be provided.

(2) The pen or pencil should be held in a position which is most naturally comfortable. The usual position is between the thumb and first two fingers, but this may be varied.

(3) The paper may be positioned straight for hooked writing, or at an angle for non-hooked writing . . . whichever works best.

(4) Unlined, plain paper is less inhibiting for lefties.

(5) Fast-drying ink should be used. So should materials specially designed for left-handed writers: fountain-pen nibs and reversed spiral-bound notebooks (see our catalog section at the end of this book), for example.

Legibility is the prime concern here. Assistance should be aimed simply at making the mechanics of writing easier for the lefty. Speed will come later. Both legibility and speed will be helped by instructions in some of the publications listed in our bibliography: the *Text-Manual for Remedial Hand-writing*, *A Writing Manual for Teaching the Left-Handed*, and *Teaching Left-Handed Children* are all recommended.

Some children between the ages of five and nine are occasionally discovered doing mirror writing before they are taught otherwise. What's more, they can usually read without difficulty what they have written. Many children tend to reverse some letters of the alphabet, and to write, for example, Ƨ instead of S and И instead of N. But true mirror writing is the reversal of the shape of every letter, and the backwards spelling of all words, which are written from right to left across the page. Only when held up to a mirror does the writing become legible to most of us.

Did you know...

...that a lefthanded teacher may have a great advantage? When learning sports and manual skills, righthanded students can face and imitate a lefty instructor as if they were looking in a mirror.

To most right-handed adults, and to lefties who have been taught conventional writing in school, mirror writing seems a difficult feat. (Try a simple sentence for yourself—or tackle our crossword puzzle at the end of this chapter.) But some lefties may find mirror writing quite easy with only a little practice. It is a pattern of writing which seems to come most naturally when done with the left hand. Some of the people who have been observed, over the years, doing mirror writing have been right-handed victims of accidents or war: after losing use of their right hand, they tried writing with the left—and the results, to everyone's surprise, came out in mirror image.

The fascinating theory is that each hemisphere of our brain registers identical images, but that the image in the non-dominant hemisphere is reversed, as seen in a mirror. People who have cross-dominant brain patterns, like most lefties and many ambidexterous folk, may have a particularly strong tendency to store images of writing in the conventional pattern in one hemisphere and in mirror image in the other.

The most famous mirror-writer in history is the Italian artist and engineer, Leonardo da Vinci. Most of his drawings and his mirror writing (he wrote entire volumes in mirror script) were executed with his left hand. Because of his notebooks filled with mirror writing, Leonardo was accused of attempting to hide "criminal, heretical thoughts about Nature and God." Another famous mirror-writer was Charles Lutwidge Dodgson, who under the pseudonym of Lewis Carroll wrote *Alice's Adventures in Wonderland* and its sequel, *Through the Looking-Glass and What Alice Found There.*

Except when it is a game played by children who have already mastered conventional writing, you want to prevent your offspring from mirror writing, of course. The first step is to train the youngster to write from left to right, instead of in the opposite direction (which comes most naturally to a lefty). Experts suggest having the student trace letters to reinforce the desired direction. Another technique is for the teacher to make marks on blank writing paper, clearly indicating the starting point and the direction in which the words are to be written.

Your lefty child is less likely to have difficulties with arithmetic than with reading or writing. But if problems do come up, teachers in your school system may be interested in experimenting with the very newest system of teaching this subject. It replaces conventional mathematics and the New Math (with all its even Newer variants), but it is, in fact, the very oldest system of all—you use your fingers for counting. It's an ancient system with a new twist, and it may be particularly helpful for a lefty child who is, almost inevitably, very aware of his or her hands.

JABBERWOCKY

'Twas brillig, and the slithy toves
Did gyre and gimble in the wabe:
All mimsy were the borogoves,
And the mome raths outgrabe.

She puzzled over this for some time, but at last a bright thought struck her. "Why, it's a Looking-glass book, of course! And, if I hold it up to a glass, the words will all go the right way again."

This was the poem that Alice read.

JABBERWOCKY

'Twas brillig, and the slithy toves
Did gyre and gimble in the wabe:
All mimsy were the borogoves,
And the mome raths outgrabe.

Mirror writing reverses the shape of every letter and spells all words (which are written from right to left) backwards. Only when held up to a mirror does it become legible for most readers. (From **Through The Looking-Glass** *by Lewis Carroll).*

Chisanbop is the name of the new system, which was developed in Korea about twenty years ago. The two hands are used, in effect, as a kind of simplified, miniature abacus. Each finger is assigned a numerical value: the four fingers of the right hand each count as 1, and the right thumb has the value of 5, while the four left-hand fingers are each worth 10, and the left thumb counts as 50. By pressing down combinations of ten fingers and thumbs, you can add up to a total of any number between 1 and 99.

Try it, while looking at the illustrations.

Let's say that you are asked to add 7 and 16. First, make the number 7: with your right hand, press down the thumb (5) and the first finger (1) and the second finger (1). Now you want to add 16—which you need to think of as 10 + 5 + 1. Add the first unit of 10 by bending down the index finger of your left hand. Now you need to add the next unit: 5. Do this by making a small exchange between the two hands: first, lift up or subtract your right thumb (which has been counting for 5), then, add or lower the second finger on your left hand (which has a unit value of 10), and you will have a net gain of 5. The final 1 is added by putting down the third finger of your right hand. What's the answer? —23 (that's 10 + 10 + 1 + 1 + 1). It's much easier than it sounds. Increasing numbers of schools may adopt the Chisanbop method as manuals and workbooks on addition,

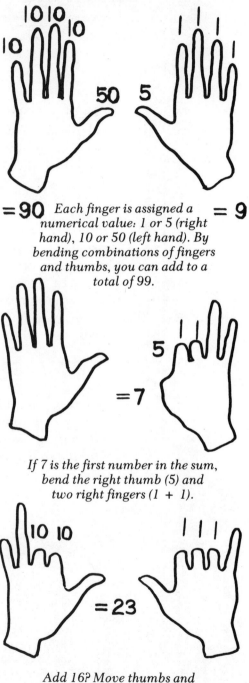

The Chisanbop system of adding.

Each finger is assigned a numerical value: 1 or 5 (right hand), 10 or 50 (left hand). By bending combinations of fingers and thumbs, you can add to a total of 99.

If 7 is the first number in the sum, bend the right thumb (5) and two right fingers (1 + 1).

Add 16? Move thumbs and fingers of that value, and you'll get the answer: 23.

subtraction, multiplication and division are published by the group called Chisanbop Enterprises Inc., P.O. Box 37, Bronxville, NY 10708.

Once problems with Reading, 'Riting and 'Rithmetic have been successfully solved, a lefty child may have fun with mirror writing and may turn out to be unusually good at games and puzzles that involve transposing or rearranging letters.

Take the name of the most famous of all French lefties: NAPOLEON. How many shorter words can your children (or you) make out of the letters that spell his name? NAP, POLE, ON, NO, LOOP, LOPE, NEON . . . these are just a few.

"Able was I, ere I saw Elba," lefty Napoleon might have mourned, when he was exiled in defeat to that island. He never said it (he spoke French!). But his words form a perfect palindrome.

Chances are that the lefties will score higher than the right-handed members of your family, because they have a natural tendency to look at letters from right to left as well as in our conventional arrangement.

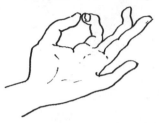

Many puzzles and contests involve anagrams—words formed by re-ordering all the letters of another word.

EON can become ONE, APE can be turned into PEA, and so on. A palindrome is a particular kind of anagram: a word which reads exactly the same even when its letters are precisely reversed. Some examples are PEEP, DEED, NOON and RADAR. Entire sentences can be composed as palindromes, with a little rearrangement of punctuation and spacing between words.

MADAM, I'M ADAM, is one.

And here's another: A MAN, A PLAN, A CANAL, PANAMA!

"ABLE WAS I, 'ERE I SAW ELBA," are words put into the mouth of Napoleon—supposedly a lament about his exile to that island in 1814, and one of the best known of all palindromes.

Try some of these games and the crossword puzzle on the following page. Lefties in your family may do them surprisingly well.

This is a puzzle that will be easy only for the select few—the very small percentage of people (usually lefties) for whom mirror writing is natural.

Spell each word "backwards," from right to left; reverse the shape of each letter, as shown. For the solution, turn to page 160.

CLUES ACROSS

1 He signed the Constitution with his left hand.
4 Rounded movable object used by many well-known lefties.
6 Place to play game named for 4 Across.
9 The most anti-left people in history.
12 Ancient city once inhabited by 9 Across.
13 Possible state of a tippling lefty.
14 The great left-handed conqueror of the ancient world.
17 Face southwest: this compass point will be to your left.
18 Home state of Left Hand Plus, Inc., store.
19 Mythological princess loved by a god in an ancient pro-right culture.
21 Prohibition (on eating left-handed at a Moslem meal, for example).

23 If at first you don't succeed with this puzzle, keep up the effort.
24 King of the fairies in medieval folklore.
25 Modern way of distinguishing father from son (papa of lefty Hans Holbein the Younger, for example).
27 Baseball player Gomez.
29 Adult female bird has one only on the left.
32 Feathered vertebrate with sinistral reproductive system.
34 As in 23 Across, make another attempt.
36 Organ of vision, usually dominant on the same side as handedness.
37 He is more likely than a daughter to be left-handed.
39 Famous southpaws include a Judy, Betty,

Dorothy, Mandy, Kristy and Joey. But do you know a female lefty with *this* name?
41 Organ of hearing, more sensitive on the sinistral side for any lefty.
43 Many a mammal shows paw preference. What about an old-fashioned rabbit?
45 Lefties have good musical memory. Remember the sixth note of the scale?
46 Glass to reflect this puzzle in.
48 Prolonged sigh of satisfaction, perhaps when this puzzle is finished.
51 Therapeutic group the lefty in 13 Across might join. (2)
52 Initials of lefty actor Terence Stamp. (2)
53 American author of a pro-lefty petition. His first name is 1 Across.

55 Of or facing the left side.
58 Home of left-handed Hoosiers.
59 To buy or sell a special lefty product, place one of these.
60 Great Lake southwest of The Sinister Shoppe, Toronto.
61 Southpaw singer Carr.
63 Dick Smothers or Duke Snider.
64 Long-tailed rodents with clear paw preference.
65 Compass point to your left, when you face south-southwest and have west-north-west on your right.

DOWN

1 Nocturnal mammals that fly (to the left, of course).
2 Port in Pennsylvania, 300 miles from Waiting For Lefty store.
3 Rest, if you need it!
4 Portion of the central nervous system you are now using.
5 Egyptian city with many colossal statues of lefty Rameses II.
6 Type of foray mounted by the corrie-fisted Kerrs, perhaps.
7 Whispering in the left ear of a lefty increases this.
8 A church for the Kerr clan.
10 A degree in science might help you now.
11 A swastika, for example.
15 Left-handers' League, abbr.
16 Where the sun rises.
20 To gain knowledge and skill (hard for lefties in some schools).
22 Anableps might be caught in one.
23 Repeat 23 and 34 Across, one more time.
24 Spheres like eyes and the sun.
25 A golfing situation in which the ball of your opponent (possibly a lefty like Bob Charles) obstructs your line of play.
26 Baseball-player Cobb.
28 Less constrained or restricted (like the creative, intuitive talents of a lefty).

30 "Yes" as a corrie-fisted Kerr would say it.
31 Actual and verifiable, like differences between lefties and righties.
33 One of the twelve known moons of the planet Jupiter.
35 Monogram on Australian champion's tennis racket?
38 Homes built by the Kerrs of Scotland.
40 Illustrator and designer of this book.
42 Egyptian god of the sun.
43 Symbol for metallic element that coats trophies won, often, by southpaw athletes.
44 Fearful of sinister witches or demons, Christians would pray to this *Pater*.
46 Girls or unmarried women (who should beware of left-hand honeymoons).
47 Name of a male Kerr, probably.
48 Provencal city in the realms of lefty Charlemagne.
49 Old word for water, part of many place-names (as in Aachen, Charlemagne's birthplace and capital).
50 Being different, no two lefties are this way.
53 Beginning of an accomplished fact.
54 Writing with old-fashioned pens, unhappy lefties would smudge these fluids.
55 The way southpaw students often feel.
56 Suffix meaning a specialist or one skilled in a subject —a lefty musician or politician, for example.
57 The Reformed Right-handers' Association?
61 Federal agency headed by Mac Cleland.
62 Completed, *id est* finished!

Crossword puzzle by Ann Novotny

104

The Lefty at Work and at Play

Away from home and school, out in the big and basically right-handed world, life for a lefty can be challenging—and even dangerous.

Let's start with the simple subject of jewelry. Wedding rings, you've undoubtedly noticed, are always worn on the left hand. This custom is a relic of the old superstition that the ring protects the "weak" side from evil. All very well ... until you think about the very real harm that can happen to a lefty who uses that hand to earn his or her living. If the left hand is used to operate machinery, the ring may catch and a finger could be badly injured or even removed. A good rule for both lefties and righties: wear rings, bracelets or other jewelry only on a hand or arm that never comes into contact with machinery or dangerous equipment of any sort.

What sort of work do most lefties do? No statistical studies have been done to determine the percentage of left-handers in any particular profession or line of business. If we accept the estimate that between ten and fifteen percent of all Americans are left-handed, we might guess that the same percentage is represented in every occupation in the United States. Is it? We just don't know.

Certain occupations, we do know, seem to be better suited than others to the natural creativity and brain patterns of lefties. It would make sense, in theory, if lefties became artists, architects, deep-sea divers, musicians and athletes. Righties should make better teachers, writers, mathematicians and scientists, as well as lawyers (but there are lefties Lewis Carroll, Albert Einstein, Clarence Darrow and F. Lee Bailey, among others, to refute that theory). The theory is just speculation, of

When a left-handed co-pilot gets promoted to pilot and the lefthand seat in the cockpit, he will find his job more difficult. Many controls will be at his right. A wedding ring, worn on the left hand, may be a safety hazard for lefties operating machinery in other occupations.

high proportion of lefties in medical professions may be explained by the fact that lefties in general are very determined people, used to overcoming obstacles on the way to their goals: if they choose to study medicine, therefore, they may be more likely than righties to finish this difficult course.

Another theory is that the practical aspects of medicine demand the use of both hands. A surgeon, in particular, needs to be skillful with both hands: it is sometimes almost imperative to be able to switch the scalpel from one hand to another without changing the whole angle of approach. There are frustrations, of course, for lefties working in medical careers. Most equipment, for doctors and patients, has been designed for righties. One left-handed nurse we know complains that there are no left-handed thermometers (she has learned to read them upside down). But ambidexterous lefties have a natural advantage in the field. One of our right-handed friends, now a doctor, remembers that when he was in medical school one professor suggested that the right-handed men in the class begin shaving left-handed, to master the use of their neglected hand.

In the worlds of art, music and literature, many creative lefties come into their own. Leonardo da Vinci, a genius at painting and drawing, sculpture, architecture and engineering, has been the subject of a dispute for years: he may have been a natural lefty (he wrote and drew with his left hand, but seems to

course. People have a hundred and one different reasons for choosing their careers. There are lefties in all walks of life, and there are right-handers who have become world-famous in professions that would seem best suited to southpaws.

Medicine is one field in which there may be a higher percentage of left-handed men and women than in the general population. There are enough left-handed dentists, for example, that equipment is specially manufactured for them. Some people have suggested that the apparently have painted with his right), or he may have developed ambidexterity to an extraordinary degree.

Michelangelo, Leonardo's contemporary and another many-faceted genius of the Italian Renaissance, has caused similar arguments. He was probably a lefty, but he may have been born right-handed and trained himself to be skillfully ambidexterous. (Irving Stone, right-handed author of *The Agony and the Ecstasy*, has admitted: "All the years I was researching and writing my book on Michelangelo, I always assumed he was right-handed.") It is known that Michelangelo painted with both hands. Standing or lying on scaffolding for hours at a time, as he painted the ceiling of the Sistine Chapel, he avoided muscular fatigue and cramps by switching his brushes from hand to hand. Some com-

Did you know...

. . . these famous lefties?

Bill Bradley

Marie Dionne
Senator Bob Dole

Raphael

Peggy Cass
Charlemagne
Bob Charles

Lefty Grove

Rex Harrison

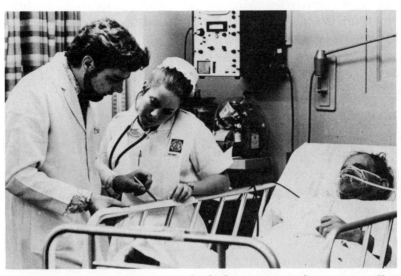

Medicine is one profession in which there seems to be an unusually high percentage of lefties.

Adam reaches out his left hand, to receive the gift of life from God. Michelangelo, who painted this and other scenes on the ceiling of the Sistine Chapel, painted with both hands and was probably a lefty.

mentators have construed Michelangelo to be left-handed because he painted Adam, in the famous scene of his creation, as extending his left hand to receive the gift of life (but God, who is bestowing this gift, is doing it with His right hand).

The British painter, Sir Edwin Henry Landseer, is another famous artist known to have been ambidexterous. Landseer was appointed to teach drawing and etching to Queen Victoria and Prince Albert— and the Queen was strongly in favor of ambidexterity, it is said. Landseer once publicly displayed an amazing ability to draw with both hands— simultaneously. At a party, he drew a horse's head with one hand, a stag's head with the other, demonstrating that his brain, eyes and hands could work with equal speed and skill on two tasks at once.

Raphael, Albrecht Dürer and Hans Holbein the Younger are listed in the roster of famous lefty artists of the first rank. So is Picasso. On the lighter side, cartoonists Milton Caniff and Reg Smyth are lefties. And so are contemporary artists Alan Cote, Robert Morris, Dorothea Rockburne, William T. Wiley, Tony Van der Meek and Charles Ross.

One classical composer of note is known to have been left-handed. He is Carl Philipp Emanuel Bach, the second of Johann Sebastian Bach's eleven sons. In his day he was more famous than his father, and known as a performer as well as a composer. Mozart and Haydn were his friends.

Two hundred years later, Cole Porter—composer and lyricist of American musical comedies—was a lefty. So are two of the Beatles, Ringo Starr and Paul McCartney.

Lefties have some advantages when they are students of music. The notes of the treble staff (those that are usually played by the right hand on a piano) are traditionally taught first. The next step is to learn the lower notes in the bass, which are nearly always played with the left hand . . . and this is where lefties can often sail easily through a stage

Two of the four-man group, The Beatles, are lefties: Ringo Starr (rear) and Paul McCartney (front left), photographed in New York in the 1960s.

that seems difficult for righties. The final lesson is to put the two hands together, with the right hand normally playing the melody while the left provides harmonious accompaniment.

Left-handed musicians may instinctively perform with better balance between the two hands that play a keyboard or other instrument. Jazz pianist Bill Evans, a friend of the authors, is a lefty who had to struggle with his school teachers to win the right to write with his left hand. When playing golf, he putts with his left but swings with his right. When questioned about playing the piano, he said he'd never given a thought to his left-handedness . . . then agreed that it probably is an asset, because most lefties have an edge over righties in any activity involving the use of both hands.

Famous pianists and violinists have been left-handed—but not always by choice. One of the best known was the Austrian pianist, Paul Wittgenstein, who lost his right hand in World War I. His French friend, Maurice Ravel, excelled at piano composition and orchestration. In 1931, Ravel wrote for Wittgenstein one of his last two major works: his Piano Concerto for Left Hand. The concerto is written in a single movement. The melodic line is played by the thumb, while the four fingers of the left hand play the other notes. Listen to this cleverly composed piece of music with your eyes closed, and you will find it hard to believe that one hand alone can create such a full, rich sound. Some critics even declare that, when the piece is played by a two-handed pianist who rearranges the fingering, the music sounds inferior. Ravel wrote that he had composed this concerto "not so much to show what the left hand can do, but to prove what can be done for the appendage that suffers from sinistral stigma."

Another famous one-handed pianist was Geza Zichy, a Hungarian count who lost his right arm in a hunting accident when he was only fourteen years old. He perfected a style of playing the piano with only his left hand. Sometimes, however, his performances were *three*-handed: he arranged Franz Liszt's "Rakoczy March" (from the "Hungarian Rhapsody" No. 15) for a three-handed duet and persuaded the Hungarian composer-pianist to play it with him on many occasions. Zichy was (on his own) an active recitalist and composer; his compositions include a whole book of piano studies for left hand alone, to which Liszt contributed a preface. Yet another one-handed player was the German composer and writer about music, Hermann von Waltershausen (born in 1882), who lost his right arm (and foot) when he was a boy. A French left-hand pianist, Charles Gros, gave successful recitals in

Paul Wittgenstein, Austrian pianist, lost his right arm in World War I. Ravel composed his Piano Concerto for Left Hand for him. By World War II, Wittgenstein was still a professional performer.

London in 1899. Willem Coenen, who was born in Holland in 1837 and died in Italy in 1918, was an unusual pianist and composer who gave performances throughout North and South America (he settled in Dutch Guiana) as well as in London. Coenen had full use of both hands—but he enjoyed fame for his left-hand performances and published piano music for the left hand only.

Cyril Smith, an English pianist, proved that righties can triumph, too. The left side of Smith's body was paralyzed after a stroke in 1956; playing with his right hand only, he returned to the concert stage to perform three-handed duets with his wife, Phyllis Sellick.

Many pieces in the single-hand repertoire were written as practice exercises to strengthen the left hand of all pianists, or as a *tour de force* on the composer's part, or (as in the case of Ravel and Wittgenstein) as special commissions for one-armed players.

Nineteenth-century piano music for the left hand includes a Sonata by Friedrich Wilhelm Kalkbrenner, a German pianist and teacher who was a friend of Chopin. Johannes Brahms arranged Bach's Violin Chaconne for a left-handed pianist. The Russian composer Alexander Scriabin wrote a Prelude and a Nocturne for left hand, and Leos Janacek—Czechoslovakian conductor, teacher, student of folk tunes, author and composer—found time to produce a Capriccio for left-hand piano and wind quintet. Another many-talented Czech, Franz Schmidt (born in Bratislava in 1874), wrote a delightful series of variations for piano, left hand alone, and orchestra. Erich Korngold, born—you've guessed it—also in Czechoslovakia (Moravia, then) in 1897, wrote a left-hand piano concerto.

The most famous composer of lefty music in our century is the German giant, Richard Strauss, who took themes from his Domestic Symphony (his fifty-third opus, written in 1903) and rearranged them in the concerto-like Parergon, composed in 1925. In Russia, Serge Prokofiev in 1931 wrote his Fourth Piano Concerto (curiously, also his fifty-third opus) specifically for one-armed Paul Wittgenstein. Benjamin Britten of

England wrote Diversions on a Theme for orchestra and left hand for pianist Harriet Cohen, who badly cut her right hand on broken glass. His fellow countryman Sir Arnold Bax has composed a Concertante for the same combination of piano and orchestra. Norman Demuth, born in England in 1898, has composed concertos, symphonies, choral music, chamber music, operas, ballets, incidental music for plays . . . *and* a Concerto and a 'Legend' for left-hand piano and orchestra.

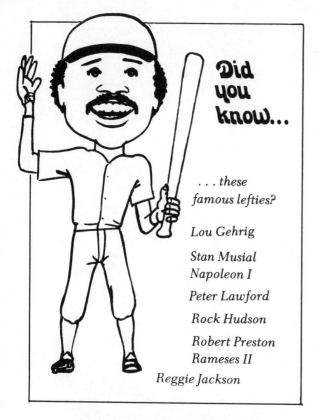

...these famous lefties?

Lou Gehrig

Stan Musial
Napoleon I

Peter Lawford

Rock Hudson

Robert Preston
Rameses II

Reggie Jackson

A colorful personality in the New York City musical world, before his death there in 1938, was Polish-born Leopold Godowsky—world-famous pianist, a great teacher, and a much admired composer of piano music. In the summer of 1935, he published a magazine article pleading for fuller cultivation of the left hand by both-handed players. The left-hand music Godowsky published included Six Waltz Poems, Six Miniatures, a Suite, and a Prelude & Fugue.

Enough! (Although there *is* more left-handed music that might be listed.) What about the one-handed righties? As Cyril Smith discovered, pianists who lose the use of their left hands can find very little music written for the right hand only. The

19th-century French composer, Charles Alkan, wrote music for the right hand, and the work of York Bowen, an English composer born in 1884, includes a Caprice for right hand as part of his Curiosity Suite. Music for the left hand only is much easier to write, because the thumb is in a position to play the treble melody. Almost the only solution for a right-handed pianist is to do as Smith did: form a duo with a two-handed performer and give three-handed recitals. It's a clear case of discrimination against righties. Perhaps a lefty composer should be generous enough to even the score and write some new piano music for the right hand?

Musicians who play stringed instruments —violins, 'cellos, banjos, guitars—normally use the left hand for fingering the strings and the right hand for bowing, strumming or plucking. If they are lefties, they may have a natural advantage over righties: the left hand has to be agile, quick and precise as its fingers hit the strings.

But some lefties suffer from an uncomfortable feeling that they are playing their stringed instrument backwards. Elizabeth Cotton, guitarist and blues singer (composer of the classic, "Freight Train"), solves this problem very simply: she holds her guitar or banjo upside down, so that the bass strings are on the bottom or lower side of the instrument. Lefties are inventive people. It is possible to restring any instrument so that it can be played in mirror image to the righty's posi-

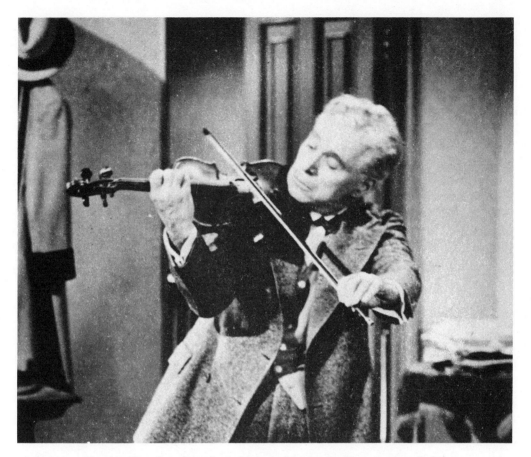

Charlie Chaplin played a lefthanded violin (with strings and chin rest reversed) in the film **Limelight**

tion. With a violin, for example, the order of the G, D, A and E strings is reversed, the pegs holding the upper ends of these strings are switched and reinserted, a slight readjustment needs to be made to the supporting wooden bridge over which the strings pass, and, finally, the chin rest is moved so that the violin can comfortably rest against the right shoulder.

Charlie Chaplin is, for most people, probably the most famous of all lefty violinists. Millions of people have watched him play the violin widdershins in a scene from the film "Limelight." That performance was no fake. Chaplin studied the violin and 'cello seriously, and for some years he dreamed of becoming a professional performer. He was one of the first musicians to have his instruments restrung so that he could play them more naturally, and in his youth he used to practice four to six hours per day, in the hope of becoming good enough to be a concert artist. Another well-known lefty violinist was Austrian-born Rudolf Kolisch, who injured his right hand in a way that prevented him from easily holding a bow in it. He reversed positions, played successfully for almost twenty years, and formed the Kolisch Quartet (disbanded 1939).

What about lefties in the other arts? There aren't too many who have devoted their lives to literature —perhaps just because the mere act of writing was a tedious business for so many lefties, before the invention of the typewriter. But the roster does include Sir James Barrie of England, as well as Thomas Carlyle (he was a reluctant lefty—he lost the use of his right hand at age 75, after a lifetime of writing). Dr. Samuel Johnson is supposed to have been a switched lefty. Americans range from Jessamyn West to Jim Bishop. And there's always Michelangelo (who was a good poet, too).

Lewis Carroll (the Rev. Charles Lutwidge Dodgson) wrote with his right hand, but there is no doubt that he was a "switched" lefty. His appearance and mannerisms support this theory. Martin Gardner writes in his introduction to *The Annotated Alice* that "Carroll was handsome and asymmetric—two facts that may have contributed to his interest in mirror reflections." Gardner goes on to describe Carroll: "One shoulder was higher than the other, his smile was slight askew, and the level of his blue eyes not quite the same. He was of moderate height, thin, carrying himself stiffly erect and walking with a peculiar jerky gait." His

physical problems seem clearly to be those of a switched lefty, or of a person suffering from extreme cross dominance. According to Gardner: "He was afflicted with one deaf ear and a stammer that trembled his upper lip. Although ordained a deacon . . . he seldom preached because of his speech defect. . . ."

Carroll may have had troubles, and he certainly had eccentricities, but—like many lefties—he possessed a number of different talents. As well as being a deacon in the Church of England, he was a mathematician (he taught that subject at Oxford University), a photographer, a poet of humorous verse, the inventor of a variety of mathematical and verbal puzzles, and, above all, an unexcelled story teller. We remember him, more than a century later, for the stories he published as *Alice's Adventures in Wonderland* (1865) and *Through the Looking-Glass* (1872), although these are not his only books.

Carroll's books are filled with the jokes, puzzles and tricks in which he so delighted. They contain palindromes, for example, and a strong awareness of the left and right sides of many things (such as the White Knight's brain, and the mushroom that Alice nibbles on one side to grow larger, on the opposite side to become smaller). In *Through the Looking-Glass* Carroll presents his readers with mirror writing and with an entire mirror world. The identical twins, Tweedledum and Tweedledee, are mirror images of each other; Alice goes in the wrong direction in the train, and she walks backwards to meet the Red Queen. It's significant that one of Carroll's own preliminary sketches for one of his two later *Sylvie and Bruno* books shows the character called Peter, seated at a big desk, using a quill pen as he cheerfully signs a bond—left-handed!

One more skill of Carroll's was his ability to draw. Even though he was no great artist, he had the knack of drawing double pictures which (somewhat like a visual sort of palindrome) looked exactly the same, whether they were held right way up or upside down.

Lewis Carroll was undoubtedly a natural lefty. One of his own sketches of a character called Peter (created after Alice) shows Peter writing with a quill pen—lefthanded.

Writing, music and art . . . these and other fields have engaged many famous (and slightly-less-than-famous) lefties, who work and play in them as professionals or as talented amateurs. But in no activity are lefties as visible as in sports. All spectators—friends and family, fans in the stadium, viewers at their television set—notice at once when an athlete picks up a bat, racket or club and swings it lefthanded. If you're a lefty, an athlete yourself or just an enthusiast, you probably know already that many lefties excel at sports.

The baseball field is where the word southpaw was coined, as noted before. Around 1890, a newspaper sports reporter (possibly Finley Peter Dunne of *The Chicago News* or Charles Seymour of *The Chicago Herald*) invented the name that has become a synonym for lefty.

Baseball is a sport in which lefties have a clear advantage. A lefty at bat swings in a way that leaves him one step closer to first base and even propels him in that direction. Southpaw batters have become legends. Babe Ruth, whose name means "baseball" to everyone, began his career as a southpaw pitcher, then switched to the outfield so that he would be able to bat every day, and became the game's most famous slugger. His record of sixty home runs in one season was set in 1927, and not beaten until 1961—by another lefty, Roger Maris of the New York Yankees. Other famous lefthanded batters include Ty Cobb,

Lou Gehrig, Ted Williams, Stan Musial, and Reggie Jackson.

Lefties have made outstanding contributions to sports, and sports have enhanced the public image of the lefty. Southpaw champions are proof of the superior coordination, strength and success that all lefties can achieve. They have unusually good visual perception of depth, a clear advantage in sports such as skiing. Lefties find it easiest to excel, of course, when they need no specially-designed equipment—or no equipment at all.

Running and swimming require no equipment, just athletic coordination and skill. Mark Spitz is a lefty. Olympic decathlon gold medalist Bruce Jenner may have made good use of the lefty's vision as he jumped those hurdles. Skiing and skating (note that Dorothy Hamill is a lefty), like tennis, squash and all ball sports, involve equipment which can be used by either hand or foot. And there are outstanding lefties in all these sports: Gale Sayers and Ken Stabler of football fame, basketball stars Bill Russell and Willis Reed, and the highest paid sports personality of our time, soccer star Pelé.

Statistics as well as legendary names seem to prove that lefties make first-class batters. Since the turn of the century, about one third of hitters have been lefties. In 76 batting championships in the National League, southpaws have won 35 times (that's 46%). In the Ameri-

Three lefties—Sandy Koufax, Ron Perranoski and Johnny Podres— with righty Don Drysdale in 1963.

Ted Williams at the plate demonstrates the advantage of being a lefty batter. As he swings from left to right, his follow-through leaves him facing first base, ready to run.

can League, lefties have captured 51 out of 76 titles (67%). That means that an overall 56% of the batting champs have been lefties. And here are more impressive statistics. Out of 63 players who have batted over .300 for ten seasons or more, 31 have been lefthanded. There were, by comparison, 29 righties and 3 switch-hitters. And 46% of the batters in the Baseball Hall of Fame are lefties. Is it any wonder that scouts for the major leagues look lovingly at a prospective little leaguer who is a southpaw?

Lefties in baseball may have been considered "screwy," but they have always been sought after. Lefty pitchers were looked for to counteract the great successes of lefty batters. In addition to throwing a batter

off balance by throwing from the other side, a lefty pitcher has no trouble keeping his eye on a runner at first base. Over 30% of all major league pitchers are southpaws. Famous southpaw pitchers include Warren Spahn, Sandy Koufax, Whitey Ford, Lefty Gomez, Ron Guidry and Tug McGraw. Out of self defense, many batters have learned to be switch-hitters, so that they can stay in the line-up against both lefthanded and righthanded pitchers.

A startling 48% of major league firstbasemen are southpaws. A lefty at first can cover a lot of infield ground with that gloved right hand of his, and he finds it easy to throw to second for that all-important double play. Alas, positions other

Lefty Gomez, one of baseball's most famous southpaw pitchers.

who thought he wouldn't be quick enough. Sportswriter Jack Cavanaugh has described Gray's style. "After catching a fly ball, Gray, using one swift, fluid motion, would bring his glove up to his right armpit, letting the ball roll down his wrist and across his chest," Cavanaugh has written. "With his glove tucked under his right stump, he would then drop his left hand in time to catch the ball and then rifle it in." Undaunted by his physical handicap, Gray has joined the ranks of those who serve as inspiration to the rest of us.

Baseball's greatest contribution to our culture, sociologists of the future may conclude, has been to rid many people of some of their prejudices against lefties. Baseball, with its admiration for (and word for) the southpaw, has spread around the world, like Coca-Cola, wherever American culture has traveled.

than first base, outfielder, pitcher or batter do not favor lefties. In fact, no one can remember a lefthanded catcher who played that position regularly (some may bat lefty, but they throw righthanded).

Perhaps no man in baseball has come closer to achieving the unique fame of Babe Ruth than Pete Gray, the One-Armed Wonder, who played professional ball for five years. In 1944, during World War II, he joined the major leagues with the St. Louis Browns and helped them to win their only World Series championship. Since childhood Pete had had to do everything with his left arm and hand: he had taught himself to catch, throw and hit a ball. In pro ball he used a 38-ounce bat, and he threw out many a runner

A southpaw batter in Korakuen Stadium, Japan. Baseball has spread around the world with American culture, helping many people to forget old prejudices against lefties.

In Britain, where baseball has never caught on, the term southpaw is used to describe a lefthanded boxer—and he is a rare bird. Throughout the history of this sport, probably as far back as the gladiators of ancient Rome, southpaws have been discriminated against. It is difficult for them to arrange matches, because other boxers' managers fear the unorthodox (and therefore often successful) style of the lefty. In the film "Rocky," the manager warns the heavyweight champ about the perils of boxing a southpaw. "He's a lefty," the manager says. "I don't want you messing with no lefthander. They do everything backwards."

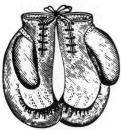

"Southpaw" means a lefty boxer in Britain, where baseball has never become popular.

What do lefty boxers do that causes their opponents so much concern? A southpaw usually leads with his right hand and foot, guarding with his left. Experts disagree on strategy against southpaws. Most believe that the opposing fighter should throw a series of right hooks to the head and body of a southpaw, because, they conclude, the blows will land on the lefty's vulnerable side. Other advisors contend that a fast left hook over the lefty's right glove is the best shot. Southpaws confound the strategists and often fell their opponents. But the outcome of "Rocky" was pure fantasy, because there has never been a lefthanded heavyweight champion in this century. There has been a light heavyweight (Melio Bettina), a middleweight and welterweight (Carmen Basilio, who fought righthanded but was a lefty out of the ring), a featherweight (Freddie Miller of Cincinnati) and a flyweight (Jackie Patterson of Scotland). About a dozen lefties in all have won world championships in divisions lighter than heavyweight, but as yet no southpaw has captured the highest honor in boxing.

Boxing is not the only sport that discourages participation by lefties. In polo—a sport in which the horses, as well as the players, must be protected from collisions—penalties are incurred for some strokes which can best be executed by a lefty. Although permitted by the American Polo Association, lefthanded play is actually prohibited in Britain and many countries of the Commonwealth, forcing natural lefties (such as Charles, the Prince of Wales) to play dextrally. The only way in which southpaws could come into their own in polo would be to assemble all-lefty teams. A fantasy!

In other sports where rules and equipment do not handicap them, lefties have become respected. Bowling and tennis, both of which have gained in popularity during the 1970s, are two such sports. A bowler competes against other players, but the game is really between the bowler, the alley and the pins. Lefthand bowling gloves and shoes are manufactured. Lefty bowlers even have a slight advantage: the right side of the lane often has a worn track or slight groove from overuse, while the left side, retaining its polished surface, is better.

Among professional bowlers, lefties account for at least 15% of the players and in recent years they

in person and on the movie screen, as "the greatest one-man bowling show on earth," a successful show-man as well as a winning competitor. At the age of 78, when his right arm and wrist began to hurt him, he started bowling as a lefty, and within two years he was averaging 180. Earl Anthony, a young lefthander from Tacoma, Washington, was named Bowler of the Year in 1974, 1975 and 1976, and he has won more than $500,000 in his career. Other well-known southpaw bowlers include Johnny Petraglia (1977 All-Star/BPAA U.S. Open champion),

Andy Varipapa, "the greatest one-man bowling show on earth," began bowling lefty at the age of 78.

have been increasing their take of the winnings, raking in 50% to 60% of the prize money.

The most famous trick of the most popular bowler of all time, Andy Varipapa, was to roll two balls simultaneously, one with each hand. His trick bowling made him known,

Jimmy Connors' powerful left arm has impressed spectators from Wimbledon to Forest Hills.

Asa Morris (the first lefty in the history of the American Bowling Congress tournament to roll a perfect game of 300), and Paula Sperber (1971 Bowler of the Year, 1975 All-Star/BPAA U.S. Open women's champ). Among non-pro lefty bowlers, the best known may be Harry S. Truman, who made good use of the White House lane.

Professional tennis players are more popular than professional bowlers, and they are wll known around the world. People who know very little about the game have still heard the names of lefties Roscoe Tanner, Rod Laver and Jimmy Connors. Young Connors, in particular, caught the imagination of sports fans from Wimbledon to Forest Hills. Winning two U.S. Open titles in three years, Connors impressed everyone with the power of his left arm.

Norman E. Brookes, Wimbledon winner in 1907 and 1914, was the first lefty tennis champion.

Other lefties among the top names in pro tennis are Czechoslovakia's Jaroslav Drobny and Martina Navratilova, Tony Roche of Australia, and Guillermo Vilas from Argentina. There's Mark Cox of Britain. And don't forget amateur Dwight Davis, for whom the Davis Cup was named in 1900. Among other amateur players, King George VI of Britain played, at championship level, lefthanded.

How many of the professional touring tennis players are now lefties? The best estimate is 18% of those on the circuit of world championship tennis—and a higher 28% of the top contenders. Tennis is a game in which a natural lefty has an enormous advantage: the righthanded opponent has to do all the adjusting. When a righthanded player sends the ball to what would normally be another righty's weak backhand, the ball is returned by the lefty's powerful forehand.

Another plus is that a lefty very often seems to be able to put more "English" or spin on the ball than a righthanded player can. This is especially useful when serving. When a lefty and a righthanded partner play doubles, they form a team that is hard to beat. By positioning themselves so that both players' forehands are on the outside of the court, they can cover the court, as Rod Laver has said, "like an octopus with a racket in each tentacle." When a lefty faces another lefty across the tennis net, all the advantages—psychological as well as physical—disappear, of course. But most players are righthanded, so lefties still have the edge (so much so that a book, *How To Play Against Lefthanders*, has been written by and for the unhappy righties who have to face them on the court).

For some reason (perhaps because lefties are only human, and enjoy the feeling of having their opponents at a disadvantage), efforts to organize an annual Left-Handed Tennis Tournament have not so far succeeded. But lefty golfers have been organized since 1934, when the National Association of Left-Handed Golfers was founded in St. Louis. The group was reorganized in 1956 and presently has its headquarters at P.O. Box 489, Camden, South Carolina 29020. The Association

describes itself as "an organization of southpaw golfers, sometimes referred to as 'the forgotton men of golf,' who are determined to prove to the world that the game was not conceived for the exclusive pleasure of right-handers." The group was founded with this purpose: "to encourage professional golfers to teach the beginner to play the game with his natural swing and to work with manufacturers in research and development of more and better equipment for lefty golfers of all ages." The Association holds a National Amateur and Open Tournament for Left-Handers, as well as a National Lefty-Righty Team Championship. Affiliated groups sponsor state and regional tournaments. For the annual dues of $12, members receive a newsletter which attempts to improve the public image of the southpaw golfer.

Lefty golfers need all the good publicity they can get. Despite the success of Bob Charles, a lefthander in the world of professional golf is still seen as an oddity. Several pros, who are lefties off the course, nevertheless play righthanded: Johnny Miller and Ben Hogan are two examples.

Why are there so few outstanding golfers who play lefthanded? Explanations range from the fact that good equipment used to be difficult to obtain, that it was even harder to find good instructors for lefties, and that lefty players used to be ridiculed by others for their apparently awkward approach to the game. As in other fields, lefties who were attracted to this sport were encouraged to switch hands in order to be effective.

The story of the ambidexterous golfer at the Montreal Club in the nineteenth century is told by the Scottish-Canadian educator and writer (and lefty), Sir Daniel Wilson: the golfer disconcerted other players by carrying *two* sets of clubs, lefthanded and righthanded. Lefty clubs were made even a hundred years ago in Scotland, the home of the game.

Another charcter in the history of lefthanded golf was an ambidexterous hustler called "Titanic" Thompson, alias "The Fat Man." He was a Texan who traveled from one golf club to another in the 1940s and 1950s, duping gullible players (often the pros themselves). Thompson would play righthanded, usually shooting in the low 70s. "Hell, let's bet some *big* money tomorrow," he would suggest at the end of the first day's play. "I'll even play you lefthanded!." Then he would add, "Of course, you'll have to spot me a few strokes." His opponent, never suspecting that Thompson could play as well, or even better, with his left hand, would generously spot him five or six strokes. When the big match took place, often for a bet of $10,000 or more, Titanic Thompson amazed everyone by shooting in the high 60s or low 70s and, with the advantage of his handicap, walking off with the money. Before word about his con game spread too wide, Titanic Thompson was the best ambidexterous golfer ever.

Did you know...

. . . That these well-known people trained themselves to become lefties, after losing use of their right hands?
Horatio Nelson, English Admiral, who lost his right arm in naval battle at Tenerife, 1797;
Thomas Carlyle, Scottish essayist and historian, who suffered a stroke at the age of 75;
Paul Wittgenstein, Austrian pianist, wounded in World War I;
Geza Zichy, Hungarian count, concert pianist and composer, injured in a hunting accident at the age of 14.

Bob Charles has made golfers sit up and take notice, too, though for completely different reasons. Millions have watched him using that famous left swing. The news is that Charles plays lefty only because he finds it an effective style. "The truth of the matter," he has confessed, "is that otherwise I'm a righthander. The only time I do things as a southpaw is when I hold an object with both hands, such as a baseball bat . . . or golf club."

This extraordinary righty who deliberately chooses to play golf lefthanded virtually grew up on the golf links in New Zealand. Both his parents were golf enthusiasts, and they taught him the game when he was a child. At eighteen, he won the

New Zealand Open, and by the time he was 21 he had traveled to the United States to play in the Phoenix Open, the St. Petersburg Open and the Masters Tournament. In 1963, at the age of 23, he won the British Open. So let anyone dare to say that a lefthanded swing is ineffective!

Due to players like Charles (who has written a book on lefthanded golf) and organizations such as the National Association of Left-Handed Golfers, manufacturers of golfing equipment have begun to explore a previously untapped market. The Ben Hogan Company produces equip-

ment for lefties. Clubs bearing the Bob Charles name are distributed by Dunlop. Lefties still don't have the wide selection available to right-handed players, but they can now find suitable clubs, in open stock. Their day is coming.

Fishing and hunting are very different from the big-name, big-money professional games of baseball, boxing, tennis and golf. But manufacturers have begun to recognize the needs of the solitary, amateur sportsman who likes to hunt, fish and walk alone in the woods. Lefty fishermen have always had an ad-

When motoring was a sport, and not just a means of transportation, American autos were (like British) manufactured for left-side driving.

vantage when it came to casting. A righthander must cast with his or her right hand, then switch the rod to the left hand in order to reel. A lefty. who has generally learned to be ambidexterous, can usually cast left and reel right. But manufacturers are now willing and able to supply lefthanded casting reels and other gear specially designed for the staunch southpaw.

For hundreds of years, there was no such thing as a lefthanded rifle. Until the twentieth century was more than half over, the lefty with a gun—whether trapshooting or skeet-

Gunsmiths did provide duplicate cheek pieces on both sides of the gun stock, in an attempt to appease frustrated lefties. Then in 1959 Savage Arms introduced the first lefthanded version of its well-known Model 110 bolt-action rifle. At last a lefty could shoot rapid fire without having to pause, to switch hands and throw a bolt. A few years later Savage manufactured a lefty 12-gauge shotgun, which ejects spent shells to the left instead of to the right. Now a number of companies make rifles specially for lefthanded hunters.

Savage Arms model 110 was (and is) the first lefthanded bolt-action rifle, introduced in 1959.

shooting, hunting for food or for pleasure, practicing marksmanship or fighting in a war—had to fire it righthanded. Southpaws had to make do with guns they had to turn upside down to load, with shotguns that had a cast off slant built in on the wrong side for them, and later with an ejection device which spat out used shells dangerously close to the user's eye. Lefty soldiers in World War I found it impossible to fire the newly developed bolt-action rifle unless they shot righthanded (as the Army decreed they must). Alterations to a bolt-action rifle owned by a southpaw sportsman in peace time were possible, but expensive.

Hunting knives, archery bows and even boomerangs are now available for the lefty. Turn to the next section of this book for a catalog of retail stores and mail-order outlets where these and other lefty items may be bought. One problem: lefty products are specialty products, and therefore they tend to be initially costly and also difficult to trade or to sell second-hand. One solution: a new news-letter, or a column in the publications of existing lefty organizations (see the next chapter, again), so that southpaws can advertise secondhand products they wish to buy or sell.

To save money and to meet friends . . . lefties, unite!

BILL MAULDIN • COLE PORTER • CLARENCE DARROW • THOMAS CARLYLE

Help is at Hand

GERALD FORD • *CARY GRANT* • *RINGO STARR* • *JUNE ALLYSON*

Lefty Organizations to Join

In the last few years, lefthanders have started to organize. Like members of all minority groups, they have seen the need for publicity and public relations to let the rest of the world know who lefties are, how they live and what special problems they face. Even a Bill of Lefts has been printed, and "Kiss Me, I'm Left-Handed" buttons are for sale.

Lefties are independent, stubborn individualists, however, and many of them are not "joiners" by nature. Several groups have been formed, have attracted a small number of members, and then—like the Society of the Left Hand founded in California—have dropped from sight. Other nations may be better at organizing their lefties: in Japan, there is reported to be a lefthanders' league with over 1,500 members.

In the United States, three groups (two of them with the word "International" in their names) are currently in existence. The International Left Handers Society has a clenched left fist as its emblem and " 'Southpaw'—I am special" as its slogan; the society is located at Box 10198, 5521 West Center Street, Milwaukee, Wisconsin 53210.

On the East Coast is The League of Lefthanders, directed by Robert Geden. The address is P.O. Box 89, New Milford, New Jersey 07646 (201 265-9110). Membership in this society, which was started in 1975, is $5 per year; members receive a quarterly newsletter. The purpose of the League is mainly educational and informational: continued efforts are made to persuade manufacturers to make left-handed items, to convince schools to buy left-handed equipment, to inform hospitals about research in brain dominance (which might be relevant to rehabilitation programs for war veterans or victims of strokes). One current campaign: to have questions on handedness included in the next U.S. census.

Lefthanders International, Inc., is in the Midwest, located at 3601 South West 29th Street, Topeka, Kansas 66614 (913 273-0680), directed by Ms. Jancy Campbell. Date of the first annual lefthanders' convention: August 10-12, 1979 (close to the annual celebration of Lefthanders' Day every August 13). Place: the Crown Center Hotel, Kansas City. Sponsors: Lefthanders International, Inc.

Annual membership dues in Lefthanders International are $15 with-in the U.S., and $18 outside the country. Two-year and three-year memberships are offered at slight reductions, and a lifetime membership costs $200. Members receive a subscription to the quarterly magazine, *Lefty*, and to the eight annual issues of *Leftyletter*, as well as a membership certificate, a wallet identification card, a "LEFTY" window sticker, and a list of retail stores and mail-order companies specializing in lefthanded products. Founded in 1975, Lefthanders International has on its board of trustees Gerald R. Ford (38th President of the United States) and Robert Dole (U.S. Senator from Kansas).

So join these or any new organization you may hear about in the near future . . . and you will find yourself in good company.

Shops, Mail-Order Catalogs and Products for the Lefty

CALIFORNIA:

A Fine Hand
2404 California Street (at Fillmore)
San Francisco
CA 94115
(415 922-9464)

Beautiful hand-crafted gifts and gadgets for lefthanders. Greeting cards, stoneware mugs, leather-bound address books and handlaced journals that open "backwards." Unusual imports and fine crafts, from around the world.

Left Hand World
Pier 39, Box P-8B
San Francisco
CA 94133
(415 433-3547)

Speciality: Karis watches, manufactured exclusively for lefthanders (color catalog available, free).

The Left-Handed Complement
4229 Noeline Avenue
Encino
CA 91436
(213 990-4226)

Unique items for lefthanded people: table and kitchen ware, T-shirts, designer-made belts created to be fastened by the lefty, scissors and writing materials, left-handed guitars and even a lefty Australian-type boomerang. Among the more prosaic but sensible items: a Hamilton Beach steam iron with the cord on the left side, and a child's ambidexterous feeding set. Catalog $1. New owner: Sylvia Marcus.

Lefty, Inc.
P. O. Box 1054
Torrance
CA 90505
(213 375-6658)

Mail order catalog, 50 cents.

The Lefty Shop
7008 South Washington Avenue
Whittier
CA 90602
(213 696-2558)

Opened and operated by Betty M. Hora, who was in her late forties before she discovered, to her astonisment, that she was lefthanded. Dedicated to the many needs of lefties. Catalog available.

COLORADO:

Southpaw Inc.
701 West Hampden Avenue
Cinderella City
Englewood
CO 80110
(303 761-8353)

Holsters and cartridge belts, bows, guns, shooting vests, baseball and softball mitts, golf clubs, all sports gloves, fishing reels, scissors, school supplies, household items, books, T-shirts and novelties . . . all for the southpaw. Write for free catalog.

CONNECTICUT:

Aristera: Left Hand People
9 Rice's Lane (P.O. Box 141)
Westport
CT 06880
(203 226-4334)

Lefty Survival Manual (catalog) available for $1, includes cartoons, letters and historical tidbits along with 80 products. Products and information to "open up a new world of gracefulness, strength, accuracy and comfort." Everything from smudge-free pens, spiral notebooks, scissors, ladles, can openers, corkscrews, playing cards and instruction books. Charge cards accepted (minimum $10). The Left Hand Man: Pete Neiman.

FLORIDA:

Kiddie Corral
Independence Square Mall
Dunedin
FL 33528

Strictly for children, a kids' boutique opened in 1978 by Ron and Kathy Seichko. The Lefthanded Corner specialities: scissors, spiral notebooks, T-shirts that say "Kiss Me, I'm Lefthanded" and "Lefties of the World Unite!"

Left Hand Ltd.
216 Northeast First Avenue
Hallandale
FL 33009
(305 454-5338)

That phone number is 454-LEFT!

Left Hander Etc.
1940-7 North Monroe Street
Tallahassee
FL 32303

The mother-daughter team of owners has organized a local lefty club.

ILLINOIS:

Left Hand Plus, Inc.
P.O. Box 161
Morton Grove
IL 60053
(312 966-3033)

Catalog available for $1.

KANSAS:

Lefthanders International, Inc.
3601 South West 29th Street
Topeka
KS 66614

The "Bill of Lefts," reproduced on 8½ × 11 inch parchment and suitable for framing, may be bought for $2 (additional copies for $1.25 each) including postage and handling.

Sitzmark Sport Shops
9339 Santa Fe
Overland Park
KS 66212
(913 381-1615)

New department sells lefthanded scissors, knives, cooking utensils, notebooks—all under $10. Manager: Steve Brace.

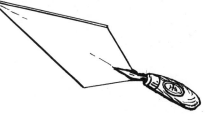

MAINE:

Left Out
17 Heather Road
Portland
ME 04103
(207 797-5277)

Catalog available. Owner: Mrs. Roberta Fishman, a righty who has two lefty children. Nearly 150 items stocked.

MARYLAND:

Lefthanded Complements
9664 Horizon Run Road
Gaithersburg
MD 20760

Catalog available.

MASSACHUSETTS:

Left-Handed Complements
P.O. Box 647
Brookline Village
MA 02147
(617 232-2822)

Owner Marcie Lewinstein, left-handed herself, selects for other lefties a practical range of kitchen utensils and tableware, a Hoover iron with the cord on the left side, sporting goods, pen and stationery, instruction and information books, 11 types of scissors. Gift certificates available. Fifteen-page catalog for $1. (Note: "complement" means "providing something felt to be lacking.")

MINNESOTA:

Left Center
4400 Excelsior Boulevard
St. Louis Park
MN 55426
(612 926-6033)

Serves the Minneapolis—St. Paul area. Co-owner Jackie Morlock, the lefty of the family, is a calligrapher, so inventory carries many pens, as well as cooking and recreational equipment, books and other items. Catalog available.

NEW YORK:

The Left Hand, Inc.
140 West 22nd Street
New York
NY 10011
(212 675-6265)

The oldest and largest purveyor of products for lefties in the U.S. Retail store; mail-order catalog (30-page) available for $1, which may be deducted from first order. Specialities: golf clubs, catchers' mitts, fishing reels, kitchen tools (such as counterclockwise corkscrews), workshop tools, books, Osmiroid and Platignum pens, T-shirts, guitars, playing cards. Also almost everything from A (address books, aprons, archery sets) to very close to Z (wallets, whimsies, wristwatches, writing instructions and yardsticks). More than 150 items designed exclusively for lefties. Since 1969. President: June Gittleson.

OREGON:

Genevieves
10129 N. E. Clackamus
Portland
OR 97220

The Southpaw
36 The Water Tower
5331 South West Macadam Avenue
Portland
OR 97201
(503 248-9877)

Orders for stock items processed within 48 hours. Items range from a grooming brush designed for lefty owners of pets to a bumper sticker reading "Left-Handed Is Beautiful." Books, mitts, mugs, scissors, pens, playing cards and a counterclockwise or reversed electric wall clock. Credit cards and gift orders accepted. Catalog.

PENNSYLVANIA:

Waiting for Lefty
Realty World Plaza
Jenkintown
PA 19064
(215 572-0313)

TEXAS:

The Southpaw, Inc.
P.O. Box 400834
Dallas
TX 75240
(214 387-2876)

Did you know... *. . . that there may be a practical reason why men's clothes have buttons on the right, women's on the left? Prosperous women, in the past, were dressed by maids (usually righthanded), so their clothes were designed to be buttoned easily by someone standing facing them. Men more often (though not always) dressed themselves, so their buttons are in the do-it-yourself position for righties.*

A lefthander's world of gifts and gadgets. Speciality: the slogan "Left Handed Genius" on tote bags, T-shirts, posters and paper weights. Other T-shirts read "I'm a Sensuous Southpaw" and "A Southpaw Superstar," while a bumper sticker asks "Honk If You're a Lefty." Send $1 for catalog (redeemable on first $5 purchase), or go in person to The Southpaw at The Olla Podrida, 12215 Coit Road No. 255, Dallas.

WASHINGTON:

Springtime Cutlery
P.O. Box 3911
Seattle
WA 98124
(206 323-7750)

Left-hand shears with natural-action left blades (not simply right-handed shears with lefty grips). Free information.

If you cannot find the item you want at these mail-order and retail stores for lefties, there's only one thing to do: adopt the tactics of The League of Lefthanders, phone or write directly to manufacturers, asking them if they make a version of their product for lefthanders—and if not, why not? Manufacturers who are thoughtful enough to produce left-handed (or ambidexterous) products should be contacted, too, with a vote of thanks from the lefties they are helping.

A few businesses who will welcome inquiries and comments from lefties are listed below.

Chisanbop Enterprises, Inc.
P.O. Box 37
141 Parkway Road
Bronxville
NY 10708

Publishers of instruction manuals and workbooks for the new Chisanbop method of learning mathematics by using the fingers of both hands.

Commuter Coffee Cup
Box 3130
Anaheim
CA 92803

A plastic mug inside a holder which is attached to a flat surface in your automobile. For no-burn, no-mess coffee on the morning drive to work. The protective lid can be rotated for left-hand or right-hand use.

Savage Arms Division
Emhart Industries, Inc.
Westfield
MA 01085

For the lefthanded sportsman (or woman), Savage manufactures the 110-CL adaptation of the 110-C bolt action center fire rifle, with lefthand stocks and actions.

Sears Roebuck and Co.
Sears Tower
Chicago
IL 60684

Through mail-order catalog or at your local Sears store, you can now buy a portable, mini drill press—the Sears Craftsman 3/8-inch Portable Variable Speed Drill Press, Model 1197—with an operating handle that can be set up on either side of the machine. Designed to bridge the gap between small hand-held drills and large industrial drill presses, this mini press is powerful enough for many home workshop projects (drum sanding, circle cutting, dowel-hole boring), yet light and small enough to move and store easily.

Wichita Engineering & Supply
333 Lulu
Wichita
KS 67211

Lefthanded models of the Classic and the Varmint rifles for hunters. Both guns come in a variety of calibers and are deluxe grade.

Travelling in other countries? Make a point of asking the local tourist office or travel agent in each city whether or not there are any local stores for lefties. Here are a few that you can visit:

AUSTRALIA:

Lefthanded Products
Box 5189
G.P.O., Sydney
New South Wales 2001

CANADA:

Forget-Me-Not Shoppe, Ltd.
232 7th Avenue, S.W.
Calgary
Alberta
(403 262-9988)

The Lefthander
P.O. Box 211
N.D.G. Station
Montreal
P. Quebec H4A 3P5

Catalog of simple, useful objects: corkscrew and can opener, scissors and pens, a reversed ruler and potato peeler, address book and posters.

Main Gauche
Box 207
Montreal
P. Quebec H4W 2Y4

The Sinister Shoppe
71 McCall Street
Toronto
Ontario M5T 2X1
(416 593-1532)

Retail and wholesale. Specialities: an exclusive lefties-only knife with natural wooden handle, and leather key cases. Complete cutlery collection.

ENGLAND:

Anything Left Handed, Ltd.
65 Beak Street
London W1
(01 437-3910)

Located half way between Oxford Circus and Piccadilly Circus in central London. Kitchen and tableware, scissors for children and for adults, Osmiroid and other pens, watches, stationery, electric irons with reversed cords, tools, pottery (including a "Lefty" mustache mug).

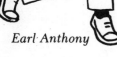
Earl Anthony

Famous Lefties to Remember

George Burns

A **Dan Ackeroyd** (television actor in "Saturday Night Live");

Eddie Albert (Edward Albert Heimberger, actor, born 1908);

Alexander the Great (4th-century B.C. monarch and conqueror of Greece, Egypt and the Persian Empire);

George Allen (head football coach: L.A. Rams, Washington Redskins);

June Allyson (actress, born New York City, 1923);

Donny Anderson (football player with Green Bay Packers, born 1949);

Gary Anderson (world target rifle champion);

Earl Anthony (three-time Bowler of the Year);

B **Carl Philipp Emanuel Bach** (composer, 1714-1788, Johann Sebastian Bach's second son);

*****Lord Baden-Powell** (Robert Stephenson Smyth, British soldier, founder of the Boy Scouts in 1908);

F. Lee Bailey

F. Lee Bailey (lawyer, born in Massachusetts, 1933);

Sir James M. Barrie (1860-1937, Scottish author of *Peter Pan*);

Carmen Basilio (welterweight prize fighter from 1948 to 1961);

Bob Bergland (U.S. Secretary of Agriculture);

Alphonse Bertillon (19th-century French criminologist);

Melio Bettina (Italian-American light-heavyweight world champion of 1939);

***Aneurin Bevan** (1897-1960, Welsh socialist leader of Britain);

Billy the Kid (William H. Bonney, 19th-century bandit);

Jim Bishop (American writer);

Robert Blake (actor, born 1933, known as "Baretta" on television);

Vida Blue (baseball player, San Francisco Giants);

The Boston Strangler (Albert H. DeSalvo, murderer);

Bill Bradley (basketball player and U.S. Senator);

George Brett (baseball player, Kansas City Royals);

Louis Brock (baseball player, St. Louis Cardinals, born 1939);

Norman E. Brookes (Wimbledon tennis champion, 1907 and 1914);

Lenny Bruce (comedian);

McGeorge Bundy (Ford Foundation president, national security advisor);

Carol Burnett (comedian, born Texas, 1936);

George Burns (Nathan Birnbaum, comedian, born in New York City, 1896);

Sir Cyril Burt (British psychologist and educator);

George Bush (head of U.S. Central Intelligence Agency);

Ruth Buzzi (actress and comedian, born Connecticut, 1936);

Brendan T. Byrne (Governor of New Jersey).

Robert Blake

James Corbett

Charlie
Chaplin

Sid Caesar

Julius Caesar (Roman general, historian and dictator, assassinated in 44 B.C.);

Sid Caesar (comedian, born Yonkers, N.Y., 1922);

Mike Caldwell (baseball pitcher for Milwaukee Brewers);

Milton Caniff (cartoonist, born Ohio, 1907);

Rodney ("Rod") Carew (baseball player, born Panama, 1945);

** **Thomas Carlyle** (19th-century Scottish essayist and historian);

Vikki Carr (singer, born El Paso, Texas, 1942);

*** **Lewis Carroll** (Charles L. Dodgson, English author of *Alice's Adventures in Wonderland*);

Jack Carter (comedian, born New York City, 1923);

Peggy Cass (television panelist and comedian);

Sir Charles (Charlie) Chaplin (English actor, born 1889);

Ty Cobb

Charlemagne (742-814 A.D., Charles the Great, King of the Franks);

Bob Charles (golfer from New Zealand);

Prince Charles (Prince of Wales, heir to the British throne);

** **Max Cleland** (Administrator, Veterans Administration, lost right arm in Vietnam War);

"Ty" (Tyrus Raymond) Cobb (baseball outfielder, 1886-1961);

Natalie Cole (singer, daughter of Nat King Cole);

Denis Compton (English cricket player, bowls lefty, bats righty);

Chuck Connors (actor, born Brooklyn, 1921);

Jimmy Connors (tennis player, born Illinois, 1952);

Hans Conried (actor, born Baltimore, Md., 1917);

James ("Gentleman Jim") Corbett (19th-century heavyweight);

Angel Cordero (jockey, born Puerto Rico, 1942);

Alan Cote (American painter);

Elizabeth Cotton (folk-blues singer, song writer and guitarist);

Dave Cowens (basketball player and coach, Boston Celtics);

Mark Cox (British tennis player);

Quinn Cummings (young actress in "Goodbye Girl").

Olivia DeHavilland

Johnny Dankworth (musician and composer);

Adrian Dantley (basketball player, Los Angeles Lakers);

Clarence Darrow (1857-1938, Ohio lawyer remembered for the Scopes trial about Darwinian theory);

Dwight F. Davis (government official, donor in 1900 of the Davis Cup for tennis);

Olivia DeHavilland (actress, born Tokyo, Japan, 1916);

John Dillinger (bank robber, shot by FBI agents in 1933);

Edward III

Lou Gehrig

Elizabeth, Queen Mothe

Errol Garner

Marie Dionne (one of five quintuplet sisters, born in Ontario, 1935);

Bob Dole (U.S. Senator from Kansas);

Thomas Aloysius Dorgan (turn-of-the-century cartoonist and humorist);

Richard Dreyfuss (actor starring in "Jaws" and "Goodbye Girl");

Jaroslav Drobny (Czechoslovakian tennis player, Wimbledon champion, 1954);

Richard Dunn (British boxer);

Albrecht Dürer (German painter and engraver, 1471-1528);

Bob Dylan (singer and composer, born 1941).

Bob Eckhardt (U.S. Representative from Texas);

Edward III (King of England from 1327 to 1377);

Albert Einstein (German-born physicist, formulator of the theory of relativity);

Queen Elizabeth (the Queen Mother, widow of George VI of Britain);

Robert Ellsworth (former U.S. Assistant Secretary of Defense);

Marty Engels (comedian).

George Gobel

F

W. C. Fields (vaudeville and film actor, 1880-1946);

Peter Fonda (actor, born New York City, 1939);

Gerald Ford (38th President of the United States);

Henry Ford, Jr. (industrialist and automobile heir);

Whitey Ford (New York Yankees baseball player, born 1928);

Chuck Foreman (football player for Minnesota Vikings, born 1950);

*__Benjamin Franklin__ (American statesman, author and scientist, 1706-1790);

Neale Fraser (Australian tennis player, Wimbledon doubles champion, 1959, 1961);

Allen Funt (television producer, born Brooklyn, 1914).

g

James A. Garfield (20th President of the U.S., assassinated 1881);

Judy Garland (1922-1969, singer and film actress);

Errol Garner (1921-1977, jazz pianist);

Lou Gehrig (baseball player, died 1941);

Uri Geller (para-psychologist);

*** **George VI** (King of Great Britain and Northern Ireland from 1936 to 1952);

Euell Gibbons (naturalist, author of *Stalking the Wild Asparagus*);

Paul Michael Glaser (actor, known for role as "Starsky");

George Gobel (comedian);

Albrecht Dürer

Herbert Hoover　　　*Bruce Jenner*　　　*Ham Jordan*

Lefty Gomez (baseball player);

Tom Gorman (baseball umpire);

Betty Grable (1916-1973, actress, born St. Louis);

Cary Grant (British film actor, born 1904);

Peter Graves (actor, born 1926, known for "Mission Impossible" role);

** **Pete Gray** (one-armed baseball player for St. Louis Browns);

Lefty Grove (Robert Moses) (baseball player, 1900-1975);

Ron Guidry (baseball player, 1978 winner of Cy Young Trophy).

 Dorothy Hamill (ice skater, Olympic gold medalist);

Louis Harris (national public opinion analyst);

Rex Harrison (English film and stage actor, born 1908);

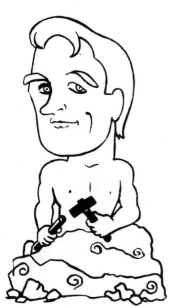

Rock Hudson

Huntington Hartford (philanthropist, art collector, A&P heir);

Tim Hauser (member of The Manhattan Transfer, all-lefty music group);

Goldie Hawn (actress and comedian, born Washington, D.C., 1945);

Ann Haydon Jones (British tennis champion, Wimbledon, 1969);

Isaac Hayes (popular composer, born Tennessee, 1942);

Jimi Hendrix (musician);

Joey Heatherton (actress, born Rockville Centre, N.Y., 1944);

Ben Hogan (lefty golfer who played right-handed);

Hans Holbein the Younger (German artist, court painter to Henry VIII of England);

Herbert Hoover (31st President of the United States);

Rock Hudson (actor born Illinois, 1925).

Daniel Inouye (U.S. Senator from Hawaii).

Jack the Ripper (murderer of 5 London women in 1888);

Kate Jackson (actress, known for "Charlie's Angels" role);

Reggie Jackson (New York Yankees baseball player, born 1946);

Bruce Jenner (Olympic decathlon track-and-field medalist);

Tommy John (baseball player, New York Yankees);

*** **Dr. Samuel Johnson** (1709-1784, English lexicographer, critic, author and conversationalist);

Randy Jones (baseball player, San Diego Padres);

Hamilton Jordan (adviser to President Jimmy Carter).

Milt Kamen (comedian);

Gabe Kaplan (actor known for "Welcome Back Kotter" role);

Danny Kaye *Michael Landon* *Hal Linden*

Danny Kaye (comedian, born Brooklyn, 1913);

Caroline Kennedy (daughter of President John F. Kennedy and Jacqueline Kennedy Onassis);

Graham Kerr (the "Galloping Gourmet");

Phyllis Kirk (actress, born New Jersey, 1930);

Paul Klee (Swiss painter and graphic artist, 1879-1940);

Kathe Kollwitz (1867-1945, German graphic artist and sculptor);

Jerry Martin Koosman (baseball player, born 1942);

Sandy Koufax (baseball player, born Brooklyn, 1935).

 * **Sir Edwin Landseer** (19th-century British painter);

Michael Landon (actor, born Queens, N.Y., 1936);

Hope Lange (actress, born Connecticut, 1933);

Paul McCartney

Rod Laver (Australian tennis player, born 1938);

Peter Lawford (English-born actor and Kennedy in-law);

Cloris Leachman (actress, comedian in "Mary Tyler Moore");

Leonardo da Vinci (1452-1519, Italian Renaissance artist, sculptor, architect, engineer and painter of the 'Mona Lisa');

Hal Linden (actor, born New York City, 1931);

Cleavon Little (actor and comedian, born 1939);

Floyd Little (football player, born 1942);

Louis XVI (King of France from 1774 to 1792, died 1793 in the French Revolution);

Allen Ludden (television master-of-ceremonies);

Sparky Lyle (baseball player, winner of 1977 Cy Young award).

m

Paul McCartney (one of the Beatles, English rock-music group);

Tug McGraw (baseball player for Philadelphia Phillies);

Robert McNamara (World Bank president, former U.S. Secretary of Defense):

Kristy McNichol (actress in ABC's "Family");

Steve McQueen (actor, born Indianapolis, 1930).

Jeb Magruder (witness in the Watergate scandal);

Marcel Marceau (French mime, born Strasbourg, 1923);

Roger Maris (New York Yankees baseball player, born 1934);

Rube Marquard (baseball pitcher, New York Giants);

Harpo Marx (1893-1964, second of the 5 Marx brothers, comedians in film and vaudeville);

Marsha Mason (actress, screen debut in "Goodbye Girl");

Ryan O'Neal

Martha Mitchell

Edward R. Murrow

Laurel Masse (member of The Manhattan Transfer, all-lefty music group);

Bill Mauldin (cartoonist of World War II, born 1921);

Anne Meara (actress);

Eddie Mekka (actor known for "Laverne and Shirley" role);

Rina Messinger (Miss Universe of 1976);

Michelangelo (1475-1564, Italian sculptor, painter, architect and poet);

James A. Michener (novelist, author of *Hawaii*, born 1907);

Karl Mildenberger (German boxer);

Ray Milland (actor, born in Wales, 1907);

Freddie Miller (world featherweight champion 1933-1936);

Johnny Miller (golfer from San Francisco, plays right-handed);

Martha Mitchell (Washington hostess, wife of former Attorney General);

Marilyn Monroe (1926-1962, film actress);

Joe Morgan (baseball player for Cincinnati Reds, born 1943);

Asa Morris (first lefty in American Bowling Congress tournament to roll a perfect game);

Robert Morris (American sculptor);

Barry Morse (actor);

Robert Morse (actor, born Massachusetts, 1931);

Edward R. Murrow (1908-1965, news broadcaster and war correspondent);

Stan Musial (baseball player, born Pennsylvania, 1920).

Anthony Newley

Napoleon I (Emperor of France from 1804 to 1815);

Martina Navratilova (Czechoslovakian tennis player, Wimbledon champion of 1978);

LeRoy Neiman (contemporary artist);

** **Viscount Horatio Nelson** (English admiral, hero of the Battle of Trafalgar, in which he died, 1805);

Anthony Newley (English actor and song writer, born 1931);

Kim Novak (actress, born Chicago, 1933);

Ryan O'Neal (actor, born Los Angeles, 1941);

Manuel Orantes (Spanish tennis player, born 1949).

Dave Parker (baseball player for Pittsburgh Pirates);

Ara Parseghian (football coach for Notre Dame, born 1923);

Napoleon

Rameses II

Bill Russell

Robert Redford

Estelle Parsons

Estelle Parsons (actress, born Massachusetts, 1927);

Jackie Patterson (Scottish world flyweight champion, 1946);

Alan Paul (member of The Manhattan Transfer, all-lefty music group);

Pelé (Edson Arantes do Nascimento, Brazilian soccer star, born 1940);

Ron Perranoski (baseball player, Los Angeles Dodgers);

Johnny Petraglia (1977 All-Star bowling champion);

Digger Phelps (basketball coach for Notre Dame);

Pablo Picasso (Spanish painter, sculptor, graphic artist and ceramist, 1881-1973);

Johnny Podres (baseball player, Brooklyn Dodgers);

Michael J. Pollard (actor, born New Jersey, 1939);
Cole Porter (1893-1964, composer and lyricist);

Robert Preston (actor, born Massachusetts, 1918);

Richard Pryor (actor and comedian in "Silver Streak" and "California Suite").

Rameses II (Pharaoh of ancient Egypt, died 1225 B.C.);

Raphael (Italian Renaissance painter and architect, 1483-1520);

Ronald Reagan (actor, Governor of California, born 1911);

Robert Redford (actor, born Santa Monica, California, 1937);

Willis Reed (basketball player and coach, New York Knicks);

Mandy Rice-Davies (witness in the Profumo scandal, Britain);

Renée Richards (tennis player and transsexual);

Don Rickles (comedian, born New York City, 1926);

Tony Roche (Australian tennis player, Wimbledon doubles champion);

Dorothea Rockburne (American sculptor);

Nelson Aldrich Rockefeller (1908-1979, Governor of New York, Vice President of the U.S.);

Bill Russell (basketball player and coach, born Louisiana, 1934);

Babe (George Herman) Ruth (1895-1948, most famous of all baseball players);

Bobby Rydell (singer, born Philadelphia, 1942).

Babe Ruth

Gale Sayers

Eva Marie Saint (actress, born 1924);

Gale Sayers (football player, athletic director, Southern Illinois University);

Wally (Walter Marty) Schirra, Jr. (astronaut on Mercury 8, Gemini 6 and Apollo 7 flights);

Leopold F. ("Rick") Schmidt (president, Olympia Brewing Co.);

Hugh Scott (U.S. Senator from Pennsylvania);

Tiny Tim

Brenda Vaccaro

Rudy Vallee

Peter Scott (British naturalist, artist, gliding champion);

Ronald Searle (English cartoonist, born 1920);

Jean Seberg (actress, born Iowa, 1938);

Ronnye Sewalt (rodeo star);

Allie Sherman (football coach, born Brooklyn, 1923);

Shields and Yarnell (husband-and-wife mime team);

Janis Siegel (member of The Manhattan Transfer, all-lefty music group);

Dick Smothers (comedian, one of the Smothers Brothers team);

Reginald Smythe (English cartoonist, creator of "Andy Capp");

Duke Snider (baseball player, Brooklyn and Los Angeles Dodgers);

Gary Sobers (West Indian cricket player);

Warren Spahn (baseball pitcher, Milwaukee Braves, born 1921);

Ken Stabler

Paula Sperber (1971 woman Bowler of the Year, 1975 All-Star/BPAA U.S. Open women's champion);

Mark Spitz (swimmer, Olympic gold medalist, born California, 1950);

Ken Stabler (football player, Oakland Raiders quarterback);

Terence Stamp (English actor, born London, 1940);

Willie (Wilver D.) Stargell (baseball player, Pittsburgh Pirates);

Ringo Starr (a "Beatle," born Liverpool, England, 1940);

Rod Steiger (actor, born Westhampton, N.Y., 1925);

Casey (Charles Dillon) Stengel (baseball player and manager, born 1891, Kansas City, died 1975).

Frank Tanana (baseball player, California Angels);

Leonard Roscoe Tanner III (tennis player, born Tennessee, 1951);

Terry Thomas (English comic actor);

Thothmes III (Pharoah of ancient Egypt, conqueror, died 1436 B.C.);

Tiberius (second Roman emperor, born 42 B.C., died 37 A.D.);

Tiny Tim (Herbert Khaury, entertainer, born New York City, 1923);

Rip Torn (actor);

Harry Truman (33rd President of the U.S.).

Brenda Vaccaro (actress, born Brooklyn, 1939);

Karen Valentine (actress, born California, 1947);

Rudy Vallee (band leader and singer, born Vermont, 1901);

Dick Van Dyke (actor and comedian, born 1925);

Andy Varipapa (All-Star bowler and showman, began bowling lefty at age 78);

Dick Van Dyke

Bill Veeck (baseball owner of Chicago White Sox);

* **Queen Victoria** (1819-1901, Queen of the United Kingdom of Great Britain and Ireland, Empress of India);

Guillermo Vilas (Argentinian tennis player, born 1952).

 Robert Wagner, Jr. (Mayor of New York City, born 1910);

Bill Wallace (karate expert);

Henry Wallace (1888-1965, Vice President of the U.S.);

John Weitz (designer of clothes, perfumes and luggage);

Jessamyn West (writer, born Indiana, 1902);

James Whitmore (actor, born White Plains, N.Y., 1921);

William T. Wiley (contemporary painter);

Paul Williams (entertainer and songwriter);

Ted Williams (baseball player, Boston Red Sox, born 1918);

* **Sir Daniel Wilson** (Scottish Canadian, president of Toronto University);

** **Paul Wittgenstein** (Austrian pianist, born 1887);

Joanne Woodward (actress, born Georgia, 1930);

Keenan Wynn (actor, born 1916 in New York City).

** **Count Geza Zichy** (Hungarian concert pianist and composer);

Jim Zorn (football player for Seattle Seahawks).

Books and Articles to Read

General-interest books about left-handedness (three current books and some old classics on the subject):

Barsley, Michael. *Left-Handed People: An Investigation into the History of Left-Handedness.* North Hollywood, Calif.: Wilshire Book Co., 1966, 1977 (distributed by Hawthorn Books). Originally published as *The Other Hand.*

DeKay, James T. *The Left-Handed Book.* New York: M. Evans & Company, Inc., 1966 (cartoons).

Fincher, Jack, *Sinister People: The Looking-Glass World of The Left-Hander.* New York: G. P. Putnam's Sons, 1977.

Gould, George M. *Righthandedness and Lefthandedness.* Philadelphia: Lippincott, 1908

Parson, Beaufort Sims. *Lefthandedness: A New Interpretation.* New York: Macmillan, 1924.

Wile, Ira S. *Handedness, Right and Left.* Boston: Lothrop, Lee and Shepherd Co., 1934.

Wilson, Sir Daniel. *The Right Hand: Left-Handedness.* London and New York: Macmillan & Co., 1891.

Books with some sections of special relevance to lefthandedness:

Brown, Barbara B. *New Mind, New Body.* New York: Harper and Row, 1974.

Calder, Nigel. *The Mind of Man.* New York: Viking Press, 1970.

Ferguson, Marilyn. *The Brain Revolution.* New York: Taplinger Publishing Co., 1973.

Fincher, Jack. *Human Intelligence.* New York: G. P. Putnam's Sons, 1976.

Hertz, Robert. *Death and The Right Hand.* New York: Free Press, 1960.

Sagan, Carl. *The Dragons of Eden.* New York: Ballantine Books, 1977.

Books on education and "how-to" instruction for lefties:

Basic Crochet for Left-Handers. Stamford, Conn.: Marketing Plus, 1977.

Charles, Bob. *Left-Handed Golf.* Englewood Cliffs, N.J.: Prentice-Hall, 1965.

Citarella, Joseph A. *Left-Handed Crochet.* New York: The Left Hand Inc., 1973.

Clark, Margaret. *Left-handedness; Laterality Characteristics and Their Educational Implications.* (Scottish Council for Research in Education, publ. 39). London: University of London Press, 1957.

Clark, Margaret. *Teaching Left-Handed Children.* Mystic, Conn.: L. Verry, 1974. (Originally published New York: Philosophical Library, 1961).

Clarke, Nicholas. *Left Handed Guitar.* New York: Bold Strummer, Ltd., 1974.

Crochet. By the editors of Sunset Books. Menlo Park, Calif.: Lane Publishing Co., 1975.

Gardner, Warren H. *Left Handed Writing Instruction Manual.* Danville, Ill.: The Interstate Printers and Publishers, 1958.

Gardner, Warren H. *Text-Manual for Remedial Handwriting.* Danville, Ill.: The Interstate Printers and Publishers, 1966.

Gottlieb, Harry. *Golf for Southpaws.* New York: A. A. Wyn, 1953 (the publishing house no longer exists, but you may find this book in a library).

Hilden, Lenette. *Knitting Instructions for the Left-Handed,* 1971 (available from Aristera, P.O. Box 141, Westport, Conn.).

Hurlburt, Regina. *Left-Handed Knitting.* New York: Van Nostrand Reinhold Co., 1977.

Hurlburt, Regina. *Left-Handed Needlepoint.* New York: Van Nostrand Reinhold Co., 1972.

Knecht, Gabriele. *Learn To Crochet.* New York: Columbia-Minerva Corp., 1976.

Knitting. By the editors of Sunset Books. Menlo Park, Calif.: Lane Publishing Co., 1976.

Myers, Carole Robbins. *Primer of Left-Handed Embroidery.* New York: Charles Scribner's Sons, 1974.

Needlepoint. By the editors of Sunset Books. Menlo Park, Calif.: Lane Publishing Co., 1977.

Newton, Margaret, and Michael Thomson. *Dyslexia: A Guide for Teachers and Parents.* London: Hodder and Stoughton, 1975.

Phillips, Mary Walker. *Step By Step Knitting.* New York: Golden Press, 1967.

Plunkett, Mildred B. *A Writing Manual for Teaching the Left-Handed.* Cambridge, Mass.: Educator's Publishing Service, 1967.

Richardson, Nina K. *Type With One Hand.* Cincinnati: South-Western Publishing, 1959.

Sayles, Shirley. *Step-By-Step Stitchery.* New York: Golden Press, 1976 (distributed by Western Publishing Co.).

Schwed, Peter. *Sinister Tennis: How To Play Against and With Left-Handers.* Garden City, N.Y.: Doubleday & Co., 1975.

Slater, Elaine. *The New York Times Book of Needlepoint.* Quadrangle/The New York Times Book Co., 1974.

Sosin, Mark, and Lefty Kreh. *Practical Fishing Knots.* New York: Crown Publishers, 1972.

Stewart, Earl, Jr., and Harry Gunn. *The Left-Hander's Golf Book*. Mateson, Ill.: Greatlakes Living Press, 1976.

Tyler, Daniel. *Left-Handed Knitting*. New York: The Left Hand Inc., 1975.

Books for children:

Lerner, Marguerite Rush. *Lefty: The Story of Left-Handedness*. Minneapolis: Lerner Publications Co., 1960.

Silverstein, Alvin, and Virginia Silverstein. *The Left-Hander's World*. Chicago: Follett Publishing Co., 1977.

Books by and for those interested in the science of lefthandedness (anatomy, psychology, etc.):

Blau, Abram. *The Master Hand*. New York: American Orthopsychiatric Association, 1946.

Blau, Abram. *The Sinister Child*. Washington, D.C.: American Psychological Association, 1974.

Bruner, Jerome S. *On Knowing: Essays For The Left Hand*. Cambridge, Mass.: Belknap Press of Harvard University Press, 1962 (distributed by Atheneum).

Corballis, Michael C., and Ivan L. Beale. *The Psychology of Left and Right*. New York: John Wiley & Sons, 1976.

Dimond, Stuart, and J. Graham Beaumont, eds. *Hemispheric Function in The Human Brain*. New York: Halsted Press, 1973 (distributed by John Wiley & Sons).

Gardner, Martin. *The Ambidextrous Universe*. New York: New American Library, 1969.

Hecaen, Henry, and Julian DeAjuriaguerra. *Left-Handedness: Manual Superiority and Cerebral Dominance*. New York: Grune & Stratton, Inc., 1964 (distributed by Harcourt Brace Jovanovich).

Needham, R. *Right and Left: Essays on Dual Symbolic Classification*. Chicago: University of Chicago Press, 1974.

Ornstein, R. E. *The Nature of Human Consciousness*. San Francisco: W. H. Freeman, 1973.

Penfield, Wilder, and H. L. Roberts. *Speech and Brain Mechanisms*. Princeton: Princeton University Press, 1959.

Sarnat, Harvey B., and Martin G. Netsky. *Evolution of The Nervous System*. New York: Oxford University Press, 1974.

Magazine articles of general interest

American Home. "On the Other Hand," by J. Johnston. Sep. 1977.

British Journal of Psychology. "Handedness and the Pattern of Human Ability," by Edgar Miller. Vol. 62, no. 1, 1971.

British Journal of Psychology. "Handedness in Children of Two Left-Handed Parents," by Marian Annett. Vol. 65, no. 1, 1974.

Family Health. "The World of the Dyslexic Child," by Louise Clarke. Oct. 1974.

Field and Stream. "On the Other Hand," by Richard Starnes. June 1976.

Horizon. "The Lobal Society of Southpaws," by James T. DeKay. Summer 1974.

House Beautiful. "For The Lefty," by Sue Nirenberg. April 1974.

McCall's. "When Your Child Can't Read," by Kenneth L. Woodward. Feb. 1973.

Mechanics Illustrated. "Are Left-Handers All Right?" by Nino LoBello. Oct. 1969.

Newsweek. "The Left-Handers." Feb. 13, 1967.

Newsweek. "Left Hand, Right Hand," by Jean Seligmann. Sep. 8, 1975.

Popular Mechanics. "Making Life Easier for Lefties," by J. F. Pearson. June 1971.

Popular Science. "It's a Clumsy World for Lefty," by W. S. Griswold.

Psychoanalytic Review. "But Why Do They Sit on the King's Right in the First Place?" by G. William Domhoff. Winter, 1969-1970.

Psychology Today. "The Hand is Faster Than the Eye, Especially if You Read Backwards," by Jack Horn. Nov. 1975.

Psychology Today. "Southpaws—How Different Are They?" by Jeannine Herron. Mar. 1976.

Psychology Today. "Southpaws: How Different Are They?" (Letters to the Editor). June 1976.

San Francisco Examiner & Chronicle. "The Lefthanded Troubles." Dec. 3, 1972.

San Francisco Sunday Examiner & Chronicle. "By Right We Should Have More Lefties," by Dolores Katz. June 1, 1975.

Science. "Fifty Centuries of Righthandedness: The Historical Record," by S. Coren and C. Porac. Vol. 198, no. 4317, 1977.

Scientific American. "On Telling Left From Right," by Michael C. Corballis and Ivan L. Beale. March 1971.

Science Digest. "Astounding Facts About Left-Handedness," by Nino LoBello. Apr. 1960.

Science News. "Sinister Psychology," by R. J. Trotter. Oct. 5, 1974.

Science News. "Hooked Handedness and the Brain." Oct. 16, 1976.

Science News. "The Right Brain: Surviving Retardation." Oct. 8, 1977.

Science News. "Musical Pitch for Left-Handers." Feb. 11, 1978.

Time. "Lefty Liberation." Jan. 7, 1974.

U.S. News & World Report. "New Findings About Left-Handed People." June 20, 1977.

❦ ❦ ❦ ❦ ❦ ❦ ❦ ❦ ❦ ❦

Many other articles on left-handedness may be located through subject indexes to

Many other articles on left-handedness may be located through subject indexes to magazines, such as *The Readers' Guide to Periodical Literature*, available in almost every library. Depending on what you're looking for, you may want to look at specialized indexes such as the *General Science Index* or those that will refer you to articles in journals on education or psychology.

Any comments on this book? Your reactions would be welcomed, and so would personal experiences, questions, and additions to the lists of well-known lefties and lefty stores.

Write to the authors: James Bliss and Joseph Morella, c/o Communication Ventures, 23rd floor, 600 Third Avenue, New York, NY 10016.

Acknowledgements and Picture Credits

Thanks are due to the many people who helped during the preparation of this book. The following provided reprints and research material: Dr. Theodore H. Blau (Tampa, Florida), Dr. Diana Deutsch (University of California, La Jolla), Frank Elder (Executive Secretary-Treasurer, National Association of Left-Handed Golfers), Dr. P. Flor-Henry (Alberta Hospital, Edmonton), R. Gur (University of Pennsylvania, Philadelphia) and Dr. Jeannine Herron (University of California, San Francisco).

Acknowledgment is made to *The Christian Science Monitor* for permission to quote "The Rightness of The Left" by Andreas de Rhoda (Nov. 30, 1977), copyright ©1977 The Christian Science Publishing Society, all rights reserved.

Caricatures and illustrations commissioned for this book were drawn by Robert H. Yahn.

Special gratitude is expressed to Dover Publications, Inc., for the storehouse of illustrations made available through publication of the Dover Pictorial Archive Series. Picture sources in this Series were: Blanche Cirker, *1800 Woodcuts by Thomas Bewick and His School*; Edmund V. Gillon, Jr., *Picture Sourcebook for Collage and Decoupage*; Jim Harter, *Harter's Picture Archive for Collage and Illustration*; Jim Harter, *Women: A Pictorial Archive from Nineteenth-Century Sources*; Clarence P. Hornung, *Handbook of Early Advertising Art*; Ernst Lehner, *Symbols, Signs and Signets*; Eleanor Hasbrouck Rawlings, *Decoupage: The Big Picture Sourcebook*.

Other Dover books gratefully acknowledged as sources of illustrations are Ernst Haeckel, *Art Forms in Nature* (p. 57 top); Theodora Menten, *Ancient Egyptian Cut and Use Stencils* (p. 24 bottom left, p. 26 top); Zelia Nuttall, *The Codex Nuttall: A Picture Manuscript From Ancient Mexico* (p. 38 top); Walter L. Strauss, *The Complete Engravings, Etchings and Drypoints of Albrecht Dürer* (p. 28, p. 39 top).

Sources of the other illustrations are: AMF Bowling Products Group (p. 120 left); British Museum (p. 70, p. 85); Culver Pictures (p. 121, p. 124); Joel Gordon (p. 80, p. 107 bottom); Indiana University, Lilly Library (p. 115); Anne M. Irvin, Fort Collins, Colorado (p. 53); Library of Congress Prints and Photographs Division (p. 41, p. 64); Frances Lichten, *Folk Art Motifs of Pennsylvania*, Hastings House (p. 63, from original in Philadelphia Museum of Art); Magnum Photos (p. 32 top by Marc Riboud, p. 69 by Eve Arnold, p. 106 by Erich Hartmann, p. 118 by Werner Bischof); Joan Menschenfreund (p. 68 bottom); National Library of Medicine (p. 68 top); New York *Daily News* (p. 77 top, p. 77 bottom, p. 82 bottom, p. 83, p. 109, p. 116, p. 117); New York Public Library Picture Collection (p. 9 top, p. 15 top, p. 24 top left, p. 24 center, p. 24 bottom right, p. 26 center, p. 29 bottom, p. 30 top, p. 34, p. 37 bottom, p. 38 center, p. 38 bottom, p. 48 center, p. 52 center, p.54, p. 67 top left, p. 98, p. 103 bottom, p. 108); New York Public Library Prints Division (p. 77 center right); Penguin Photo (p. 113); Savage Arms (p. 125); V.J. Stanek, *Introducing Monkeys*, Artia Publishing (p. 56 top); Trinity College, Cambridge (p. 39 center); U.S. Army (p. 36 bottom); U.S. Postal Service (p. 74); Wide World (p. 67 bottom right, p. 89, p. 110, p. 118 top, p. 120 bottom); Eugene Woolridge (p. 60).

Solution to the mirror-writing crossword puzzle on page 104.

Hold the solved puzzle up to a mirror. This is what you should see.

Bob Yahn